C000186185

#CENTURIONS

PREMIER LEAGUE CHAMPIONS 2017/18

#CENTURIONS

PREMIER LEAGUE CHAMPIONS 2017/18

Sport Media

Lead Photographer: Victoria Haydn
Additional photography: Tom Flathers, Getty Images
Writer: David Clayton
Production Editor: Roy Gilfoyle
Design: Colin Sumpter, Colin Harrison
Cover design: Graeme Helliwell
Stats: SAP and Premier League
Thanks to: Matt McNulty, David Griffin, Serena Gosling
and everyone at Manchester City Football Club

First published in Great Britain and Ireland in 2018 by
Sport Media, Third Floor, 5 St Paul's Square, Liverpool, L3 9SJ.

www.tmsportmedia.com
@SportMediaTM

1

Hardback ISBN: 9781911613206

Printed by Replika

Outdoors
Thank you
YAYA
ONLY
CITY
CHAMPIONS

Premier League
Premier League
Premier League
Premier League
MANCHESTER
CITY

CONTENTS

Premier League

ETIHAD

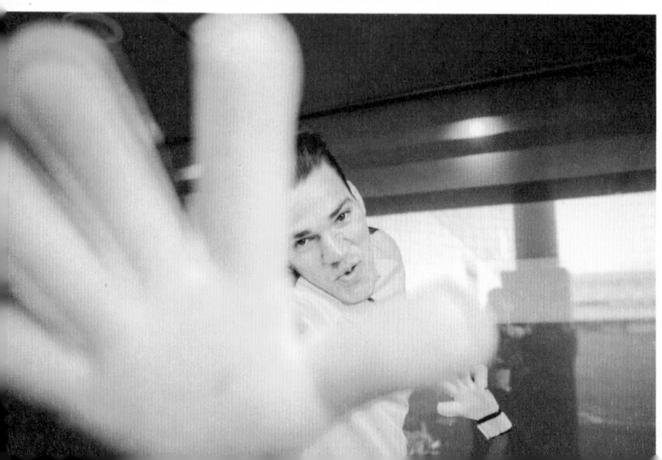

DE BRUYNE
17
10
25

MANCHESTER
CITY

Premier League
Premier League
Premier League
League

An unforgettable season for the Centurions

It took Pep Guardiola just a year in English football to figure out a system that would work best for the players at his disposal.

Having identified the players he felt he needed to improve the squad, the Blues recruited Ederson, Kyle Walker, Danilo, Benjamin Mendy, Bernardo Silva and Aymeric Laporte.

He then took the remainder of his squad and improved them as players before ensuring each squad member knew what was expected of them in the various adaptations and systems employed by the manager.

The end result was what every City fan had dreamed of – beautiful football played at the highest level and in a fashion never before seen by the Premier League.

The Blues swept all aside as Club and Premier League records tumbled, eventually culminating in a season when City were labelled 'Centurions' for reaching 100 Premier League points and over 100 Premier League goals.

City would drop just 14 points all season, winning more games than any other club in Premier League history, scoring more goals and acquiring more points than any other side had ever managed.

It was all masterminded by Pep Guardiola and his coaching staff, and performed by an extraordinary group of players who managed to win both the Carabao Cup and the Premier League in 2017/18.

This book is a tribute to the manager and all the players who contributed to the title-winning campaign.

"I am so happy and excited. It's a pleasure to work here," said Pep, who penned a new two-year contract extension at the end of the record-breaking campaign.

"I enjoy working with our players every day and we will try to do our best together in the coming years. As a manager, you have to feel good to be with the players – and I feel good.

"I will focus on the desire of my players to become a better team and every day that's what I will try to do – to improve on the pitch and improve our players.

"We have a young squad with an average age of 23 and we want to keep taking steps forward and maintain the levels we've achieved this season."

Fasten your seatbelts, Blues, because the boss believes this group of players can get even better...

RECORD BREAKERS

While the statistical focus after such an amazing season largely fell on the 100 points City managed to guzzle up, there were so many records that tumbled that it's worth reminding ourselves of them...

RECORD!
Most points

City became the first team ever to reach 100 points in a Premier League season.

RECORD!
Most goals

City scored 106 Premier League goals in total, breaking Chelsea's 103 record, set during the 2009/10 campaign.

RECORD!
Most wins

City won an incredible 32 matches in the Premier League - two more than Chelsea from the 2016/17 campaign.

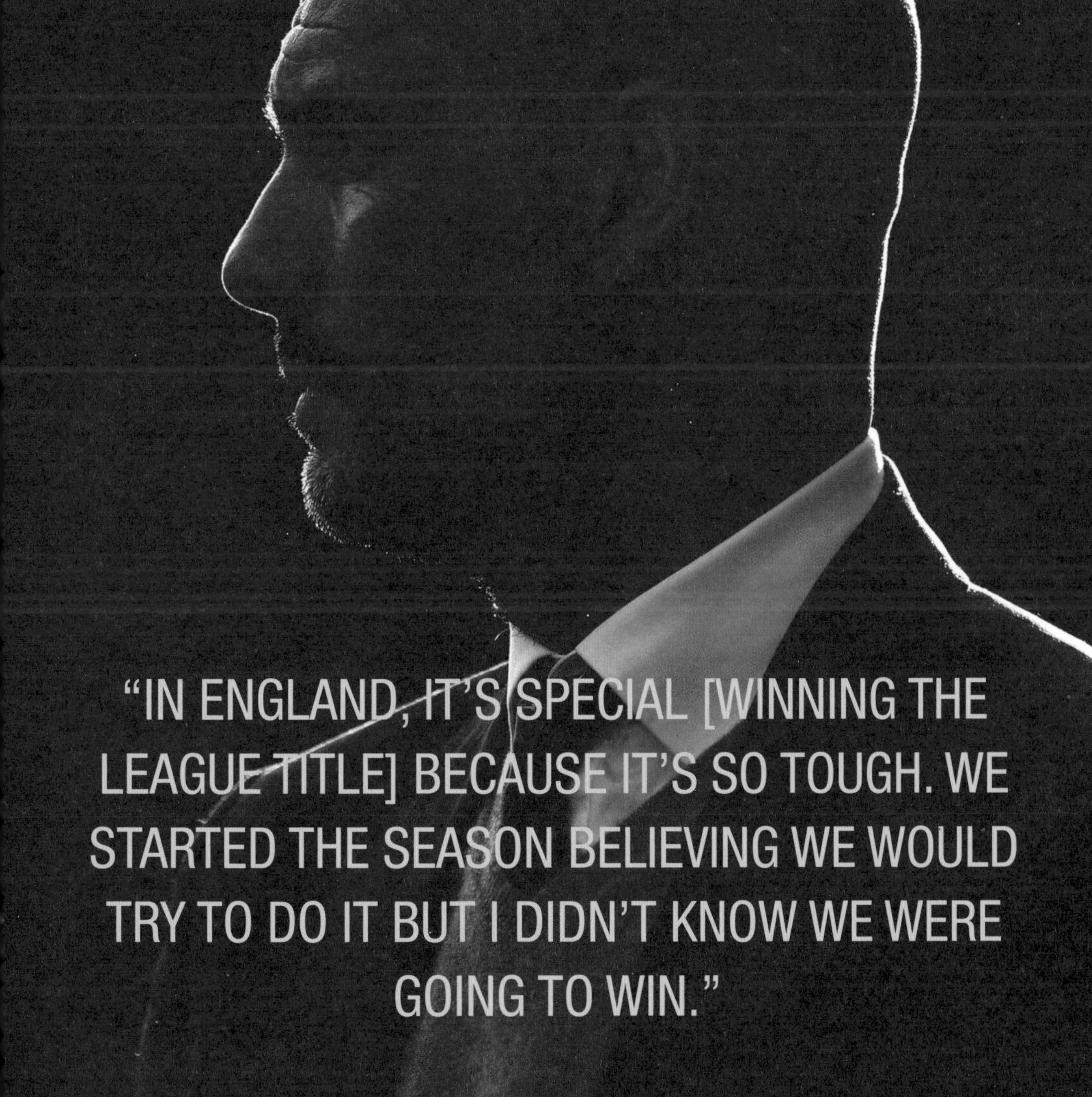

“IN ENGLAND, IT’S SPECIAL [WINNING THE LEAGUE TITLE] BECAUSE IT’S SO TOUGH. WE STARTED THE SEASON BELIEVING WE WOULD TRY TO DO IT BUT I DIDN’T KNOW WE WERE GOING TO WIN.”

RECORD!
Biggest winning margin

The Blues finished the season an incredible 19 points ahead of second-placed Manchester United, beating the Reds' 16-point margin from 1999/2000.

RECORD!
New Club record

The previous Club record of 31 wins from 2001/02 in a single season was eclipsed last season – and it is even more impressive given that was a 46-game season!

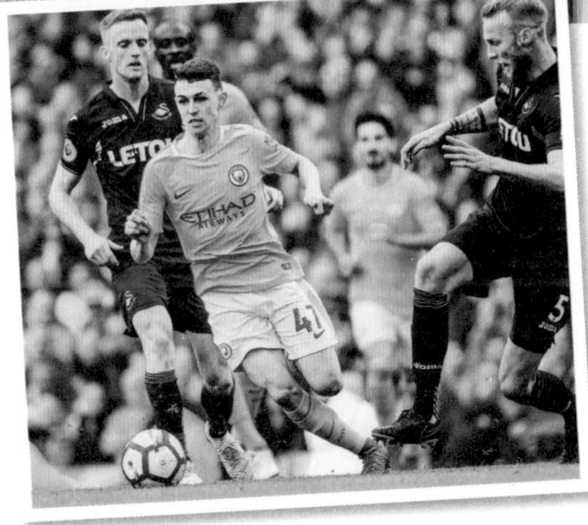

RECORD!

Youngest champion

Phil Foden became the youngest ever player to receive a Premier League medal when City were crowned champions.

ETIHAD
AIRWAYS

ETIHAD
AIRWAYS
ETIHAD
AIRWAYS
17

DE BRUYNE
17

RECORD!
Successive wins

City's 18-match winning streak before the New Year smashed the Premier League record of successive wins.

RECORD!
Most away wins

City's away points totalled 50 and included 16 wins and two draws with just one defeat.

RECORD!
Most opponents beaten

City beat every team in the Premier League at least once during the 2017/18 season, becoming only the third team in history to beat every other side in the league in the season.

RECORD!
Most possession

City's 82.1% possession stat against Everton in March 2018 is the highest ever recorded.

RECORD!
Earliest title win

City's title win with five games to go equals the record set by Manchester United in 2000/01.

RECORD!
Biggest goal difference

City finished with a goal difference of +79, beating Chelsea's previous high, set in 2009/2010.

"BACK-TO-BACK TITLES IN THIS LEAGUE WILL BE TOUGH...BUT WE ACCEPT THE CHALLENGE"

MANCHESTER
CITY

Carabao ENERGY DRINK
Premier League

VINCENT KOMPANY

For much of the first half of the season, Vincent Kompany was forced to watch City sweep all before them from the sidelines as he recovered from a series of frustrating injuries.

With the Blues playing some of the best football the Premier League has ever seen, it must have been almost unbearable for the skipper not to be involved.

He stayed patient and refused to allow the set-backs to affect him and remained as much a leader off the pitch as he is on it.

His reward was a much more productive second half to the season when he featured regularly and when he did it was clear he is still one of the best defenders in the world.

Whenever Kompany is at the heart of City's defence, the Blues look unbeatable and it was fitting that the skipper was able to lift the Premier League trophy for a third time, making him the Blues' most successful captain ever.

At one stage, with City needing to beat Manchester United to secure the title, it looked as though it might be a fairy-tale come true for the Belgian as he rose for a corner and powered a header past David De Gea to put the Blues ahead – just as he had done when the axis of the most dramatic title race in history swung City's way when his goal settled the Manchester derby back in 2011/12.

It was almost a carbon copy of that goal – as was the celebration – but United recovered to win 3-2 on the day, denying Kompany an incredible end to his tenth year with the Club.

However, it would end happily as City wrapped the title up the following weekend and the captain added the Premier League crown to the Carabao Cup winner's medal he'd won a couple of months earlier – his eighth trophy win with the Blues.

Hopefully, there will be many more to come for this genuine Manchester City legend.

ETIHAD STADIUM
CITYZENS

ETIHAD
AIRWAYS

CITYZE

IRWAYS

CITYZENS
CITYZENS

“THIS TITLE IS WHAT IT FEELS TO BE A CHAMPION. YOU ARE ALWAYS THE CHAMPIONS IF YOU WIN IT ON GOAL DIFFERENCE OR BY ONE POINT, BUT IF YOU WIN IT LIKE WE DID, IT CANNOT BE DISCUSSED. THAT IS A VERY NICE FEELING.”

ETIHAD
AIRWAYS

HAYS
ETIHAD STADIUM

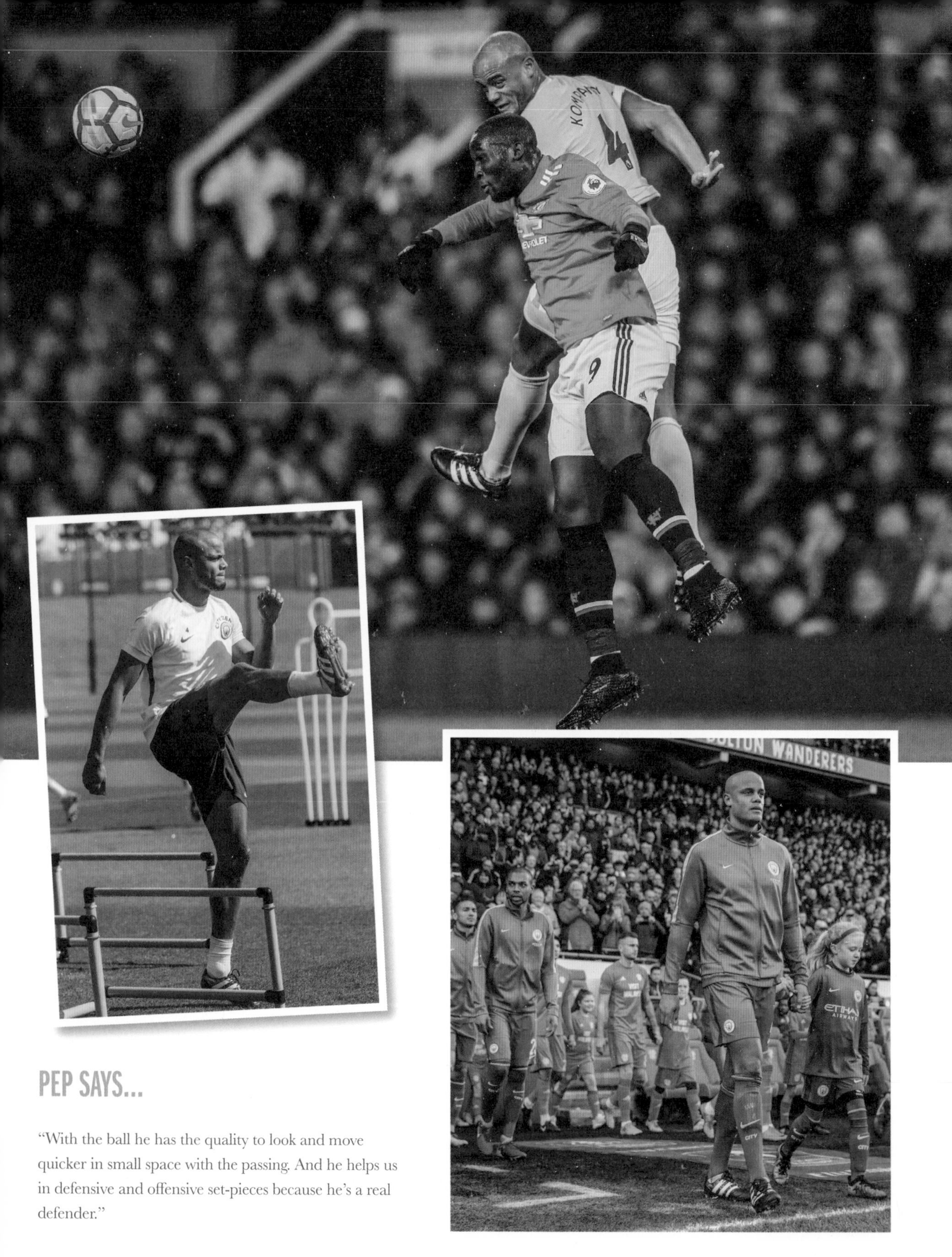

PEP SAYS...

"With the ball he has the quality to look and move quicker in small space with the passing. And he helps us in defensive and offensive set-pieces because he's a real defender."

STATS...

A leader and a player you need when the tough get going, Kompany turned up whenever he played. It's no coincidence that his two goals came in two of the Blues' biggest games of the campaign in the Carabao Cup final against Arsenal and in the potential title-winning derby against United. After 10 years, his influence is still huge.

VINCENT KOMPANY	
Position:	Defender
Date of birth:	10 April 1986
Place of birth:	Uccle, Belgium
2017/2018	(all competitions)
Appearances	20
Goals	2
Assists	1

0-1
CARABAO CUP FINAL
WEMBLEY STADIUM
MANCHESTER CITY
ETIHAD
AIRWAYS

KYLE WALKER

Signed from Tottenham in the summer of 2017, Kyle Walker was the swashbuckling right-back Pep Guardiola wanted for his attack-minded formation.

With Club legend Pablo Zabaleta bidding an emotional farewell, the Blues had no experienced right-back to call upon and Guardiola prioritised two new signings to compete for the role.

Walker arrived from Spurs and Danilo, a versatile full-back from Real Madrid, was also recruited.

Walker had developed into one of the best full-backs in the Premier League and was an integral part of a very good Tottenham side, but he wanted to win trophies and jumped at the chance to join the Blues.

Though he was sent off on his home debut against Everton, Walker slotted into the City team seamlessly and quickly became a crowd favourite.

His pace and ability on the ball meant he would regularly pop up on the right-wing or overlap when required and the fact he made six Premier League goals for his team-mates and created six more big chances speaks volumes for his valuable attacking contribution.

He would play a total of 48 games in his first season at the Etihad and settled in so quickly, it seemed as though he had been at the Club for many years.

He would end his first season with a Premier League winner's medal and a Carabao Cup winner's medal, justifying his decision to move on from Spurs and his consistency also won him a place in England's World Cup squad.

All in all, not a bad 12 months for the Sheffield-born defender and Walker will look to add many more medals and trophies to his collection in the years to come.

优必选机器人

MANCHESTER CITY

MANCHESTER CITY
ETIHAD
AIRWAYS

ETIHAD
AIRWAYS

“I WANT TO BE THE BEST IN THE WORLD. EVERYONE WANTS TO BE THE BEST IN THE WORLD AND THAT’S WHAT I WANT TO STRIVE TO DO. WITH HIS (GUARDIOLA’S) KNOWLEDGE, EXPERIENCE, HOPEFULLY HE CAN GET ME TO THAT.”

ETIHAD
AIRWAYS

PEP SAYS...

"He's fast in front, he's intelligent, good at passing short and long, can go fast forwards and backwards. He is open-minded and when that happens anything can happen. Abidal and Philipp Lahm could play in different positions and adapt immediately, so quickly, because they were so good. Kyle is quite similar."

STATS...

Kyle played 32 Premier League games and 16 further cup fixtures. He was voted by his fellow professionals as the best right-back in the country in the PFA Team of the Year and his six assists made him one of the most productive defenders in the country.

KYLE WALKER	
Position:	Defender
Date of birth:	28 May 1990
Place of birth:	Sheffield, England
2017/2018	(all competitions)
Appearances	48
Goals	0
Assists	6

Premier League
Premier League
MANCHESTER
CITY

ILKAY GÜNDOGAN

For a player dogged by long-term injuries, the 2017/18 season was a triumph for the talented German.

Gündogan has had more than his fair share of misfortune over the past four years or so, but he managed to feature in 48 games in City's fantastic title-winning campaign – the best total of his career.

Though he made many of his appearances from the bench, the former Borussia Dortmund midfielder was an integral part of Guardiola's side, offering something different with his vision and quick-thinking.

Capable of playing as a deep-lying midfielder or as part of a three-pronged attacking midfield, Gündogan goes about his work quietly, but he is a clever footballer.

He added six goals along the way, including two away to FC Basel and one of the coolest penalties you're likely to see in the 3-1 win away to Tottenham. Again, this is a career-high for Ilkay.

That Gündogan is considered a pivotal part of the Germany squad is testament to his versatility and consistency.

In his 28th year, Gündogan will arguably be reaching his peak in the 2018/19 campaign and is likely to be crucial to City's hopes of success in the Champions League.

All in all, an impressive campaign for the Blues' No.8.

CITYZENS
CITYZENS

ETIHAD
AIRWAYS
AIA
AIA
.com

"IT FEELS GREAT NOW TO BE BACK AND PART OF THE TEAM, TO PLAY MY OWN ROLE, WHICH IS ALSO IMPORTANT. I'M ENJOYING IT AND I'M VERY HAPPY. IT'S A VERY HAPPY PERIOD IN MY LIFE AND MY CAREER AGAIN."

10

PEP SAYS...

"Gundo is an extraordinary player. Last season we missed him a lot when he was injured. Not just his goals, his personality to play, he was fantastic. I am so happy for him."

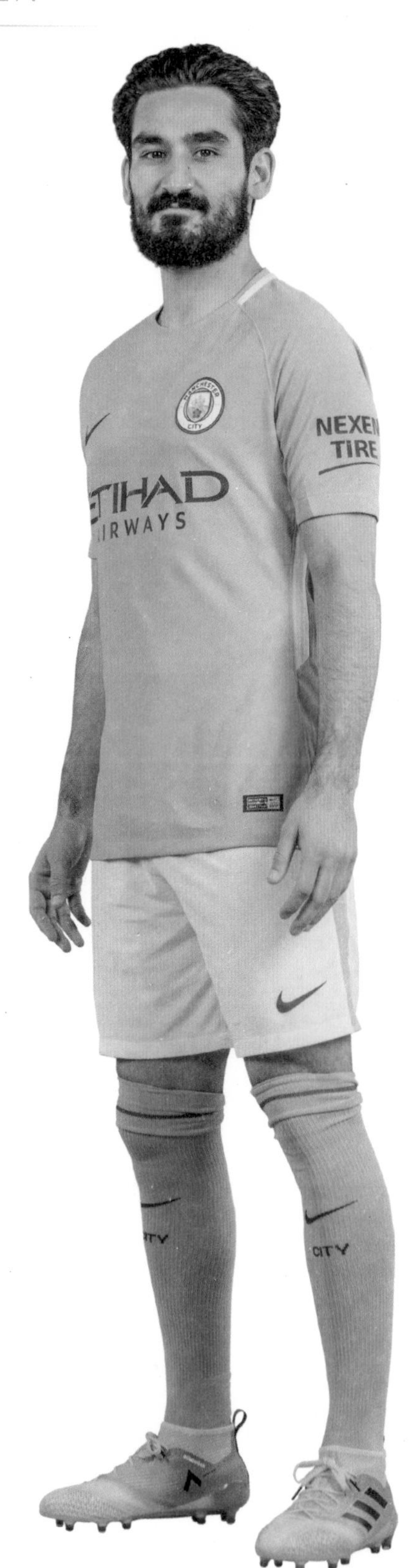

STATS...

Ilkay's total Premier League assists show that he is not in the team to create goals for others – there are enough playmakers in the team to take on that role with four of his team-mates reaching double figures. His role is to get the ball from the defence to the creative talents and patrol the centre of the pitch, break up play and defend when needed.

ILKAY GÜNDOGAN	
Position:	Midfielder
Date of birth:	24 October 1990
Place of birth:	Gelsenkirchen, Germany
2017/2018	(all competitions)
Appearances	48
Goals	6
Assists	0

EOS
EOS

17

KEVIN DE BRUYNE

As far as Manchester City fans were concerned, there was only one player who should have been crowned the PFA Player of the Year and it was Kevin De Bruyne.

While nobody could deny Liverpool's Mo Salah had an exceptional campaign, it was De Bruyne who ended the season with Premier League and League Cup winner's medals and it was De Bruyne who ended the season as the Premier League's assist king with 16.

KDB was outstanding from game one to game 38 and inspirational throughout an unforgettable campaign.

He contribution was total and you'd be hard pressed to find a more hard-working footballer in Europe.

De Bruyne was central to everything good City did and the Belgian playmaker enjoyed his most productive and exciting season yet – which is really saying something!

He featured in all but one of City's Premier League games, creating 16 goals for his team-mates including the deft lob into the path of Gabriel Jesus on the final day of the campaign that enabled the Blues to reach the 100-point mark.

Of his many unforgettable performances, his dominant display at former club Chelsea – then reigning champions – and a peach of a goal sent out a message to the rest of the Premier League that this was City's year.

In a season of incredible milestones, it was De Bruyne whose light shone brighter than any other and he was a richly-deserved winner of the MCFC Etihad Player of the Season award which he won by a landslide.

A masterful campaign from a wonderful footballer.

ETIHAD
AIRWAYS

CITYZENS

CITYZENS

Premier League

“WE ALL KNEW IF WE GOT 100 POINTS IT WOULD BE SOMETHING SO SPECIAL AND IT IS PROBABLY VERY DIFFICULT TO MANAGE AGAIN. IN THE END WE BROKE THE RECORD.”

MANCHESTER
CITY
NEXEN
TIRE
ETIHAD
AIRWAYS

PEP SAYS...

"Kevin was amazing. He is a champion. I think he will be remembered in his life, in the season 2017-18, we won the Premier League and he was fundamental to achieving that and I think that is what will make him proud the most."

STATS...

Kevin De Bruyne featured in 51 of City's matches during 2017/18, scoring 12 goals in all competitions. In the Premier League he pipped Leroy Sané for the most assists (16), made 248 crosses and struck the woodwork four times. He also made 19 'big chances' for his team-mates during a fantastic campaign.

KEVIN DE BRUYNE	
Position:	Midfielder
Date of birth:	28 June 1991
Place of birth:	Ghent, Belgium
2017/2018	(all competitions)
Appearances	51
Goals	12
Assists	16

Premier League

RAHEEM STERLING

If Raheem Sterling had managed to convert the opportunities the Premier League describe as 'big chances missed' and been luckier with the four shots that struck the woodwork, he'd have ended up with more league goals than Liverpool's Mo Salah.

As it is, he managed a career-best of 23 goals in all competitions and created 11 more in the Premier League for his team-mates in a sensational campaign for the England forward.

Raheem is unlucky because in any other season, he'd have been nailed on to land a clutch of personal awards, but he won't be complaining.

Sterling shifted up a gear this season and under Pep's guidance has become one of English football's most exciting players.

This season has seen him top all his previous stats with City and Liverpool and he was a major part of the Blues' success throughout, but it was his knack of grabbing late goals that proved so crucial.

In only the second game of the campaign, it was his late equaliser at home to Everton that prevented a damaging home defeat and it was his last-gasp winner at Bournemouth that ensured City started with momentum and purpose.

And he continued to score crucial goals all season – a late winner at Huddersfield, the only goal of a tense game at Newcastle but none better than his stunning strike at home to Southampton with virtually the last kick of the game.

And the best is yet to come – let's remember, Raheem is still only 23 going into the 2018/19 campaign.

A fantastic season both individually and for the team.

ETIHAD
AIRWAYS

ETIHAD
AIRWAYS

CITYZENS
MANCHESTER
CITY
7

ETIHAD
AIRWAYS
6

BEGOVIC
27
ETIHAD

"SCORING IS SOMETHING I'VE ALWAYS WANTED TO DO AND SOMETHING I'M TRYING TO IMPROVE ON... I'M HAPPY TO HAVE BEEN ABLE TO BRING THAT AND HOPEFULLY IT WILL CARRY ON."

CITYZENS
MANCHESTER
ETIHAD
AIRWAYS

PEP SAYS...

"The most magnificent thing is he is 23 years old, so he is still focused, keeping the desire to get better as a player. His understanding of the game is global: he's a guy who can create inside, make a movement outside, dribbling, runs in behind."

STATS...

Raheem is as much as 50% up on many of his 2016/17 Premier League stats, suggesting working with Pep Guardiola is taking his game to another level. He was getting in better positions in the box and had more confidence in his own shooting while continuing to create chances for his team-mates. Only Kevin De Bruyne and Leroy Sané provided more assists than Raheem last season.

RAHEEM STERLING	
Position:	Forward
Date of birth:	08 December 1994
Place of birth:	Kingston, Jamaica
2017/2018	(all competitions)
Appearances	46
Goals	23
Assists	11

VL-100
V-Lok

DANILO

Danilo left Champions League winners Real Madrid to join City in July 2017.

The Brazilian full-back is naturally a right-back but is comfortable at left-back and can play as part of a three-man central defence.

It was this versatility that convinced the Blues to bring him to the Etihad and, throughout the campaign, he proved he could do a job wherever and whenever he was asked.

Brazilian defenders have a well-earned reputation for being attack-minded and Danilo, like Kyle Walker, proved to be just as happy in the opposition's box as he was defending in his own.

With the typical flair that seems to be ingrained in Brazilians' DNA, Danilo would more than play his share of games for City, particularly with left-back Benjamin Mendy ruled out for the majority of the campaign with a knee injury.

By the end of his first season in sky blue, Danilo had featured in 38 games in all competitions and also scored three goals and provided two assists.

All his goals were taken with the aplomb of an accomplished striker and he's bagged a very impressive 31 goals so far in his career.

Considering he rarely had a long run of games in the team, he was consistent and dependable whenever called upon and by the end of the campaign, he'd done enough to earn himself a place in Brazil's World Cup squad – a fitting reward for the unassuming, consummate squad member.

Danilo will continue to play a crucial part in Pep Guardiola's team in the coming seasons and the two-time Champions League winner will look to add to the 12 winner's medals he already has in an impressive career collection.

PEP SAYS...

"He can play in the three at the back, he can play full-back - right or left. He can also play holding midfielder. He also knows how to handle the pressure because he's been at Madrid and Porto – clubs where every weekend you have to win. That's where his mentality comes from and that's why he's so important to us."

STATS...

Danilo is City's Mr Versatile. As a defender who likes to chip in with goals and assists, he can be pleased with his contribution of three of the former and two of the latter. When he strikes a ball, it stays hit and his goals have varied from long range strikes to lung-bursting runs into the box.

DANILO	
Position:	Defender
Date of birth:	15 July 1991
Place of birth:	Bicas, Brazil
2017/2018	(all competitions)
Appearances	38
Goals	3
Assists	2

Premier League
Premier League
Premier League
Premier League
ETIHAD
AIRWAYS
MANCHESTER CITY

35

OLEKSANDR ZINCHENKO

Oleksandr Zinchenko probably didn't expect to play much of a role in City's title-winning season.

After joining City from Ukrainian side Ufa in 2016 aged only 19, he was immediately loaned out to PSV Eindhoven and then spent time with second tier Dutch side Jong PSV.

He had little chance to impress Pep Guardiola, yet he returned for the summer and did enough to catch his manager's eye.

An attacking left midfield Ukraine international, Zinchenko trained hard, did well in pre-season and when Benjamin Mendy was ruled out for five months, Guardiola adapted the youngster to left-back as cover for Fabian Delph and Danilo.

It was a masterstroke by the boss and though Zinchenko would start just two Carabao Cup games, he was continually in and around the matchday squad and after Christmas, he was involved regularly for a spell of two months.

Each time, Zinchenko was neat and tidy and did the job he'd been asked to do with minimum fuss – impressive for a young player playing out of his comfort zone.

By the end of the campaign, he'd clocked up 14 appearances in one of the best Premier League sides of all time.

With Mendy fit, it will be interesting to see how Zinchenko is utilised next season and if he can do well in a position he's not that familiar with, the Blues may have discovered an unpolished diamond.

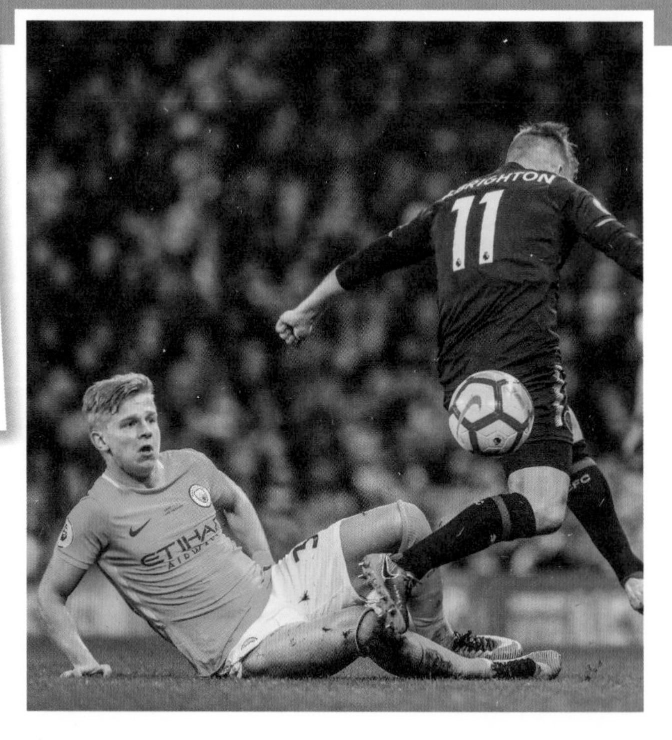

PEP SAYS...

"He is a talented player, so clear, so clean. The way he plays, his decisions are always perfect. As a young player I hope in the future he will help us."

STATS...

Zinchenko's job was to get the ball and then play it fairly simple, so while he may have no assists or goals, that wasn't what he was in the team to do. What he did was efficient and steady – he never let the team down and his efforts were appreciated by the City fans as a result.

OLEKSANDR ZINCHENKO	
Position:	Defender
Date of birth:	15 December 1996
Place of birth:	Radomyshi, Ukraine
2017/2018	(all competitions)
Appearances	14
Goals	0
Assists	0

33

GABRIEL JESUS

If Gabriel Jesus' first half-season with City had been a learning curve, his first full campaign proved what a willing student the young Brazilian was.

Jesus started the season strongly and ended it in similar fashion with only an unfortunate knee injury at the midway point hampering his progress.

Jesus was an integral part of City's Centurions season, playing 42 times in all competitions and scoring 17 goals.

Industrious and energetic, the 21-year-old works hard for the team and has enormous potential given his age.

Already a fully-fledged Brazil international, Jesus had hit double figures for goals by November and will wonder how many he might have ended up with but for the injury he sustained away to Crystal Palace on New Year's Eve.

It was 16 games before he started a match again, so to end with such impressive season stats is testament to his potential.

The Blues have only lost one of the 39 Premier League games Jesus has featured in and his goal-every-other-game ratio makes him one of the most exciting strikers in the world.

His goal-scoring form during the season run-in helped the Blues power towards a host of records and it was his cool finish with virtually the last kick of the campaign that saw City reach the 100-points mark. A fitting end to a fine season by the young Brazil star who will look to kick on again in 2018/19.

WALKER
2

CITYZENS

"I AM VERY SELF-CRITICAL AND ALWAYS WILL BE. I THINK THIS MAKES ME WANT TO IMPROVE, ALWAYS. IF I SEE THAT I DIDN'T DO WELL, I AM GOING TO WANT TO GET BETTER, ALWAYS. THIS ONLY HELPS ME OUT."

25

PEP SAYS...

"I think Gabriel never will lose his energy and it's wonderful in tandem with his quality, but with time he'll be a wiser player, he'll understand when to make that movement and another."

STATS...

With 13 Premier League goals from 29 games plus three assists – not to mention three woodwork strikes – Gabriel Jesus was a threat whenever he played. What is particularly pleasing is the way his goals are spread between right foot, left foot and headers – the mark of a true goal poacher.

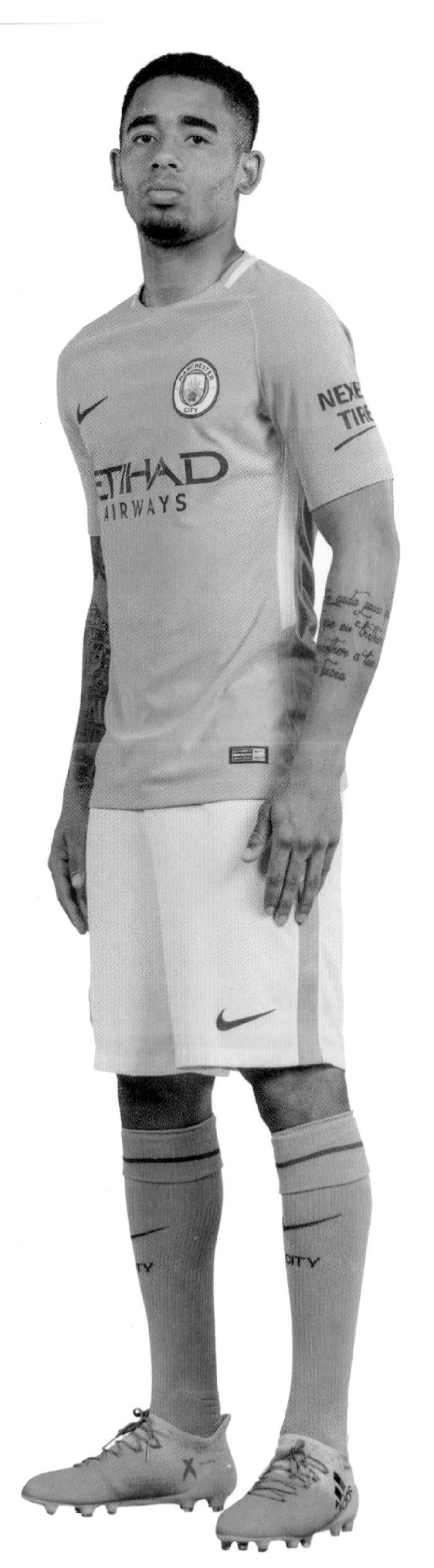

GABRIEL JESUS	
Position:	Striker
Date of birth:	03 April 1997
Place of birth:	Sao Paulo, Brazil
2017/2018	(all competitions)
Appearances	42
Goals	17
Assists	3

Premier League
Premier League
Premier League
Premier League
CITY

21

DAVID SILVA

David Silva has never let his standards slip in his eight years as a City player, but during the 2017/18 season, he took them to perhaps his best level yet.

Silva was magnificent throughout what was a very difficult period for him with his son Mateo born prematurely.

Despite his off-field concerns, Silva continued to produce the typical purring displays that have become his trademark at City.

Sporting a new shaven-headed look, Silva was at his very best from the word go, seamlessly knitting defence into attack and forging a lethal midfield partnership with Kevin De Bruyne.

Silva's intelligence, anticipation and vision were the beating heart of a team that continued to post new records on a seemingly weekly basis.

So often his stats are hidden, with Silva making the pass before the assist on so many occasions, yet the fact he scored nine Premier League goals and created 11 more for his team-mates is impressive on its own.

He also created a further 14 'big chances' during his 29 league appearances – of which City won 26 – so imagine what his stats might have looked like had he played another nine games?

Now aged 32, he was voted in the PFA Team of the Year for only the second time in eight years – so the question must be: is he getting better as he gets older?

Hopefully, the player the City fans have nicknamed 'El Mago' – The Magician – can continue weaving his magic for many more years to come.

And if he does… he might also deservedly be labelled the greatest City player of all time.

ETIHAD
AIRWAYS
G.JESUS
33
17

DE GEA
1
CHEVROLET
14
19

21
20
7

Fly Emirates

"I WANT TO SAY THANK YOU TO THE FANS, MY TEAM-MATES, THE STAFF, THE CLUB AND ESPECIALLY TO THE MANAGER FOR UNDERSTANDING MY SITUATION. TO PEP, I WILL BE INDEBTED TO YOU FOREVER."

NEXEN
TIRE
Captain
ETIHAD
AIRWAYS
ETIHAD

PEP SAYS...

"Normally people talk about his skills and technical ability and after that, he cannot be an aggressive competitor. He has both."

STATS...

It's only the second time David Silva has finished the campaign with double figures for goals. He netted 10 in all competitions from 40 appearances and his 11 Premier League assists mean that no player has created more goals since he arrived in 2010.

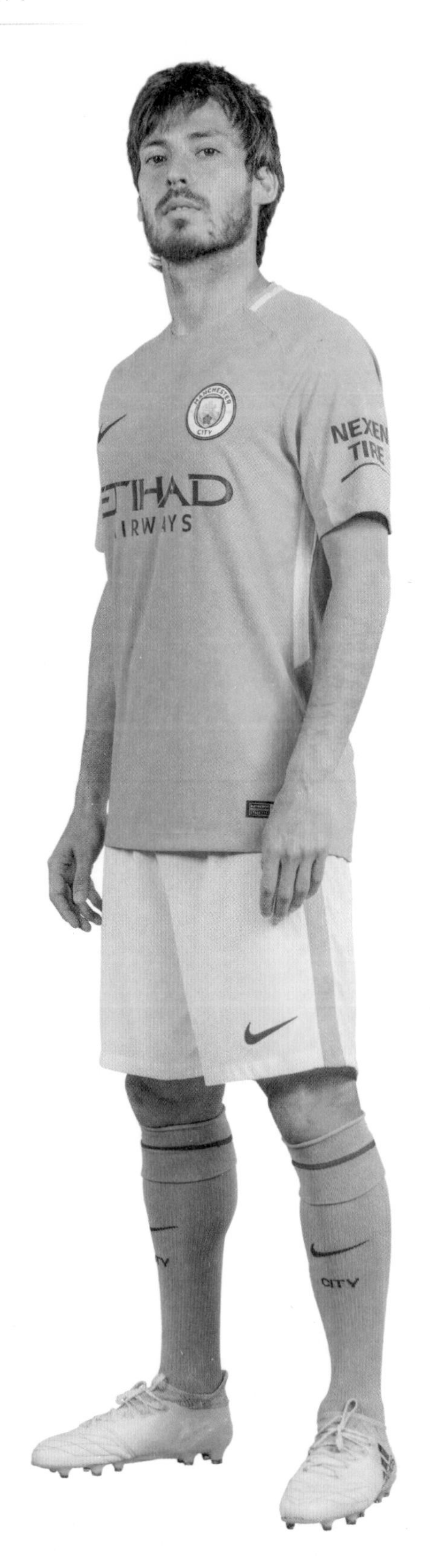

DAVID SILVA	
Position:	Midfielder
Date of birth:	08 January 1986
Place of birth:	Arguineguin, Gran Canaria
2017/2018	(all competitions)
Appearances	40
Goals	10
Assists	11

STORY OF THE SEASON

PREMIER LEAGUE CHAMPIONS

THE MARCH OF THE CENTURIONS

MATCHDAY 1

Amex Stadium, 12.08.17

BRIGHTON & HOVE ALBION 0
MANCHESTER CITY 2

Agüero 70, Dunk 75 (og)

The Blues needed to be patient against the Premier League new boys in their opening game of the season before Sergio Agüero and a Lewis Dunk own goal settled a hard-fought win. A goalless first half saw Gabriel Jesus denied at point-blank range by Seagulls goalkeeper Mathew Ryan, while the young Brazilian also saw two goals chalked off. But the strike that broke the deadlock was due in no small part to the work of Kevin De Bruyne, who won the ball on the halfway line before feeding David Silva. He threaded a pass to Agüero, who made no mistake with a clinical finish. Within five minutes, the Blues had doubled their lead after persistence by Agüero ended with Fernandinho's cross being headed past his own keeper by the unfortunate Dunk.

MATCHDAY 2

Etihad Stadium, 21.08.17

MANCHESTER CITY 1
EVERTON 1

Sterling 82 • Rooney 35

City showed fantastic resistance to earn a draw after recovering from a disastrous spell just before half-time. The home side had the better of the first half, with David Silva's shot striking a post before Everton broke the deadlock with their first effort on target, Wayne Rooney scoring his 200th Premier League goal from close range. The size of the task grew further when home debutant Kyle Walker was dismissed for two quick-fire yellow cards just before the break. But despite the numerical disadvantage, City produced an inspirational second-half performance and forced a deserved leveller through substitute Raheem Sterling's brilliantly-struck volley from Mason Holgate's poor defensive header. City pressed for a winner but it finished all square in scoreline and the number of players on the pitch, as the Toffees saw Morgan Schneiderlin sent off late on.

The players show their togetherness as they faced Everton in a tough first home game of the 2017/18 Premier League season

GOAL
19
25

Leroy Sané scored twice as City chalked up a historic result against Liverpool

PREMIER LEAGUE CHAMPIONS

THE MARCH OF THE CENTURIONS

MATCHDAY 3

Vitality Stadium, 26.08.17

AFC BOURNEMOUTH 1
MANCHESTER CITY 2

Daniels 13 • Jesus 21, Sterling 90'+7

Raheem Sterling scored a dramatic injury-time winner - and was then sent off for a second bookable offence - as City came from behind to beat a hard-working Bournemouth side. The home team drew first blood with a stunning goal by Charlie Daniels and Ederson superbly kept out Jermain Defoe from close range before Gabriel Jesus levelled the scores with a clever finish from close range. Both sides struck the woodwork after the break – Josh King for the Cherries and Nicolas Otamendi for City from Kevin De Bruyne's corner – but the Blues will feel three points were deserved given the balance of play. Bournemouth hearts were broken when a low Danilo cross was turned home by Sterling, with the winger being harshly given a second yellow card following joyous celebrations.

MATCHDAY 4

Etihad Stadium, 09.09.17

MANCHESTER CITY 5
LIVERPOOL 0

Agüero 24, Jesus 45+6, 53, Sané 77, 90+1

City took full advantage of Sadio Mané's first-half dismissal to thrash Liverpool and move to the top of the Premier League for the first time in the 2017/18 season. The Blues had already edged ahead through Sergio Agüero's opener from Kevin De Bruyne's through ball before Mane was dismissed for a dangerous kick that resulted in Ederson being stretchered off. Gabriel Jesus – who had earlier had a goal disallowed – added strikes either side of the break before a late Leroy Sané brace – the second a memorable long-range curling effort – completed the rout and ensured the Blues' biggest victory over the Reds for more than 80 years.

Sergio Agüero grabbed another City hat-trick – this time at Watford

PREMIER LEAGUE CHAMPIONS

THE MARCH OF THE CENTURIONS

MATCHDAY 5

Vicarage Road, 16.09.17

WATFORD 0
MANCHESTER CITY 6

Agüero 27, 31, 81, Jesus 37, Otamendi 63, Sterling 89 (pen)

Sergio Agüero scored a superb hat-trick as City hit Watford for six. City did most of the hard work in the opening period, scoring three goals in the space of 10 mesmerising minutes. The Argentina international showed his predatory instincts for the first two, before setting up Gabriel Jesus for the third, the 17th goal scored by the South American strike partnership in the last 10 games – and there was more to come. David Silva crossed for Nicolas Otamendi to head the fourth, before Agüero slalomed through three challenges before squeezing a low shot off the post and over the line to complete a memorable hat-trick. There was time for a brief cameo from Ilkay Gündogan, playing his first game since injuring his knee against the Hornets nine months ago. And Raheem Sterling finished off the scoring from the spot, having himself been brought down in the box.

MATCHDAY 6

Etihad Stadium, 23.09.17

MANCHESTER CITY 5
CRYSTAL PALACE 0

Sané 44, Sterling 51, 59, Agüero 79, Delph 89

Free-scoring City scored another five goals to stay top of the Premier League. Palace – who hit the post through Ruben Loftus-Cheek's low drive – held out until just before the interval when Leroy Sané broke the deadlock, and a quickfire double by Raheem Sterling (the first of them his 50th career goal) deflated the visitors' initially stubborn resistance. Late goals by Sergio Agüero – his 176th in City colours – and Fabian Delph's 20-yarder completed the rout, the first time since 1958/59 that a top-flight side has hit five or more in three successive games.

It's a picture of happiness as Kevin De Bruyne's goal put the champions to the sword at Stamford Bridge

PREMIER LEAGUE CHAMPIONS

THE MARCH OF THE CENTURIONS

MATCHDAY 7

Stamford Bridge, 30.09.17

CHELSEA 0
MANCHESTER CITY 1

De Bruyne 67

Manchester City produced their finest display of the season so far to win at champions Chelsea, a result which meant they stayed top of the Premier League table – and made it eight consecutive wins in all competitions. Kevin De Bruyne scored the winner, firing a brilliant left-footed strike past Belgium international team-mate Thibaut Courtois with just over 20 minutes remaining, and they could have added to the lead late on, with Gabriel Jesus being denied by Antonio Rudiger's clearance on the line.

MATCHDAY 8

Etihad Stadium, 14.10.17

MANCHESTER CITY 7
STOKE CITY 2

Jesus 17, 55, Sterling 19, Silva 27, Fernandinho 60, Sané 62, Bernardo Silva 79 • Diouf 44, Walker 47 (og)

City carried on where they'd left off before the international break with another blistering display, inspired by a performance of pure genius by Kevin De Bruyne, who had a hand in four of the goals. Gabriel Jesus' brace, plus goals for Raheem Sterling, David Silva, Leroy Sané, Fernandinho and Bernardo Silva undid Stoke City, who had briefly threatened a comeback with strikes either side of the break before rampant City exerted their dominance.

ETIHAD
AIRWAYS
30
CITY

Nicolas Otamendi's brave header was rewarded with a goal against Burnley

PREMIER LEAGUE CHAMPIONS

THE MARCH OF THE CENTURIONS

MATCHDAY 9

Etihad Stadium, 21.10.17

MANCHESTER CITY 3
BURNLEY 0

Agüero 30 (pen), Otamendi 73, Sané 75

Manchester City equalled their club record of 11 consecutive wins as they beat Burnley to move five points clear at the top of the Premier League table. On a historic day at the Etihad Stadium, Sergio Agüero's opener also put him joint-top of City's all-time leading goalscorer list. Bernardo Silva almost broke the deadlock before winning a penalty on the half-hour mark, which Agüero dispatched. The Argentinian twice went close to going clear of Eric Brook's record, being denied on both occasions by Nick Pope, but it was Nicolas Otamendi who doubled the advantage, heading home Leroy Sané's corner. The German raced clear soon after from Kevin De Bruyne's defence-splitting pass to finish expertly, and complete the scoring.

MATCHDAY 10

The Hawthorns, 28.10.17

WEST BROMWICH ALBION 2
MANCHESTER CITY 3

Rodriguez 13, Phillips 90+2 • Sané 10, Fernandinho 15, Sterling 64

City set a host of new records in seeing off West Brom, though this wasn't quite as comfortable a victory as it might have been. There were three goals in the first quarter of an hour: Leroy Sané thumped home, the Baggies' Jay Rodriguez nipped in to lob the ball into an empty net before Fernandinho's 20-yarder restored the City advantage. Sub Raheem Sterling swept in Kyle Walker's excellent cross just three minutes after climbing off the bench to make it 3-1. David Silva and Kevin De Bruyne should have extended City's winning margin and the Baggies pulled a late goal back through Matt Phillips to ensure a nervy last few seconds. But the victory made it a club record 13 wins in a row, 21 unbeaten – another club best.

Kevin De Bruyne opened the scoring during an important win against Arsenal

PREMIER LEAGUE CHAMPIONS

THE MARCH OF THE CENTURIONS

MATCHDAY 11

Etihad Stadium, 05.11.17

MANCHESTER CITY 3
ARSENAL 1

De Bruyne 19, Agüero 50 (pen), Jesus 74 • Lacazette 65

City extended the lead at the top of the Premier League to eight points after a hard-fought win over Arsenal. The Blues were made to fight for the points, but goals from Kevin De Bruyne, newly-crowned club record goalscorer Sergio Agüero and Gabriel Jesus were enough for a win on a day when yet more club records were broken. De Bruyne's left-footer gave City the advantage, the club's 50th goal of the season, and the lead was doubled early in the second half, Agüero making no mistake from 12 yards after Raheem Sterling was bundled over. Gunners sub Alexandre Lacazette halved the arrears but nine minutes later another sub, Jesus, hammered home from David Silva's pass to wrap up a record 15th consecutive win and the Blues' ninth successive league victory, the first time the club have achieved the feat since 1947.

MATCHDAY 12

King Power Stadium, 18.11.17

LEICESTER CITY 0
MANCHESTER CITY 2

Jesus 45, De Bruyne 49

Two moments of brilliance extended Manchester City's winning run to 16 games at the King Power Stadium. The first came when a sublime team move was finished by Gabriel Jesus just before the break. Fabian Delph and Kevin De Bruyne were involved before Raheem Sterling's pass found David Silva, who laid on the Brazilian for his 10th goal of the season. Shortly after the restart City extended their lead. After Leicester defender Harry Maguire had hit the post, City broke with pace and when the ball fell to De Bruyne, he unleashed an unstoppable, rising left-foot strike past the helpless Kasper Schmeichel. City had chances to extend the lead through Jesus and Silva, but the points were won and more club records tumbled: a 10th consecutive league victory and a seventh away win. And, crucially, another three points.

Late winners became a nice habit for Raheem Sterling

PREMIER LEAGUE CHAMPIONS

THE MARCH OF THE CENTURIONS

MATCHDAY 13

John Smith's Stadium, 26.11.17

HUDDERSFIELD TOWN 1
MANCHESTER CITY 2

Otamendi 45+1 (og) • Agüero 47 (pen), Sterling 84

City came from behind to secure victory in a blood and thunder War of the Roses. Remarkably, it was the first time in 22 years that the Blues have recovered from a half-time deficit in the Premier League, but it was arguably the hardest-fought three points of the campaign so far. An own goal by Nicolas Otamendi gave the hosts the advantage against the run of play but a penalty from Sergio Agüero, after Raheem Sterling was brought down by goalkeeper Jonas Lossl, levelled matters. Leroy Sané rattled the bar with a free-kick – but there was a touch of fortune about the winner. Sub Gabriel Jesus was denied by Lossl but Sterling, following up, saw the ball bounce off him and loop up and over the keeper into the net. Huddersfield also ended with 10 men as Rajiv Van La Parra was shown a red card after an altercation with Sané.

MATCHDAY 14

Etihad Stadium, 29.11.17

MANCHESTER CITY 2
SOUTHAMPTON 1

De Bruyne 47, Sterling 90+6 • Romeu 75

Raheem Sterling's brilliant stoppage-time winner made it 19 successive victories in all competitions, extending a club record that has helped City establish an eight-point Premier League lead with a remarkable 40 points from 14 games, the best start to a Premier League season ever. In truth, City were far from their best. Following a disjointed first half in which the visitors hit the bar from Wesley Hoedt's header, Kevin De Bruyne's free-kick broke the deadlock via a deflection off Virgil van Dijk. Gabriel Jesus and De Bruyne went close before the Blues were hit with a sucker-punch, Oriol Romeu smashing home from Sofiane Boufal's pull-back. But with the game deep into stoppage-time, Sterling curled a superb winner - his second late goal in the space of three days, one Guardiola enjoyed as he ran onto the pitch to celebrate with his players.

AIRWAYS

PREMIER LEAGUE CHAMPIONS

THE MARCH OF THE CENTURIONS

MATCHDAY 15

Etihad Stadium, 03.12.17

MANCHESTER CITY 2
WEST HAM UNITED 1

Otamendi 57, Silva 83 • Ogbonna 44

David Silva scored a late winner as City came from behind to beat a determined West Ham United side. The Blues were frustrated in the first 45 minutes and went in a goal down. Manuel Lanzini had been denied by Ederson minutes before Angelo Ogbonna rose highest to powerfully head home Aaron Cresswell's corner. Pep Guardiola responded at the break by taking Danilo off and bringing Gabriel Jesus on, and a revitalised City soon drew level. After Kevin De Bruyne's free-kick was beaten away by Adrian, City came again and Raheem Sterling's flick allowed Jesus to burst into the box and square the ball to Nicolas Otamendi, who slid home. There were chances at both ends but it was City who would celebrate a 20th successive win, De Bruyne teeing up Silva who volleyed past Adrian to send the Etihad wild.

MATCHDAY 16

Old Trafford, 10.12.17

MANCHESTER UNITED 1
MANCHESTER CITY 2

Rashford 45+2 • Silva 43, Otamendi 54

Goals from David Silva and Nicolas Otamendi earned City a priceless victory in a full-blooded, enthralling Manchester derby. The Blues took the game to a United side that were unbeaten in 40 home games, and had a 100% home record this campaign. Silva volleyed home the opener from close range, after Romelu Lukaku had failed to clear a Kevin De Bruyne corner. However, Marcus Rashford levelled moments later against the run of play after confusion in the City defence. But the Blues regained the lead in the second half through Otamendi. Again Lukaku was involved. De Bruyne's free-kick was whipped in and the United striker's clearance cannoned off Ander Herrera, with the lurking Otamendi volleying home. There were chances at both ends late on, with Ederson producing a fine double save from Lukaku and Juan Mata.

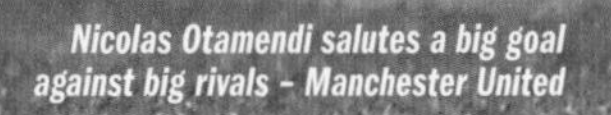

Nicolas Otamendi salutes a big goal against big rivals - Manchester United

İlkay Gündogan began the scoring against Tottenham at the Etihad

PREMIER LEAGUE CHAMPIONS

THE MARCH OF THE CENTURIONS

MATCHDAY 17

Liberty Stadium, 13.12.17

SWANSEA CITY 0
MANCHESTER CITY 4

Silva 27, 52, De Bruyne 34, Agüero 85

City returned to top form with this routine victory over struggling Swansea. Pep Guardiola's side missed a host of chances before David Silva flicked in the opener. Kevin De Bruyne's free-kick doubled the advantage before the break, and Silva made it four goals in three games minutes after he'd somehow missed when one-on-one with Lukasz Fabianski, scooping the ball over the Swans goalkeeper after good work by Raheem Sterling. Sergio Agüero completed the scoring late on and the result means City now have 49 points from 17 Premier League matches, the best start to an English top-flight campaign since the Football Association was established in 1888; better, even, than Tottenham's double-winning side of 1960/61. It also means City are the first team to win 15 successive Premier League matches.

MATCHDAY 18

Etihad Stadium, 16.12.17

MANCHESTER CITY 4
TOTTENHAM HOTSPUR 1

Gündogan 14, De Bruyne 70, Sterling 80, 90
• Eriksen 90+3

City made it 16 league wins in a row after thrashing Tottenham Hotspur at the Etihad. The Blues went ahead through Ilkay Gündogan's header and were on top for much of the game, although the points were still in the balance when the peerless Kevin De Bruyne powered forward in the area, before blasting home beyond Hugo Lloris to make it 2-0. The Belgian was brought down in the box soon after but sub Gabriel Jesus saw his spot-kick come back off a post. It mattered little though as top-scorer Raheem Sterling put the seal on matters with a late double, tapping in the first before netting through the legs of the Spurs goalkeeper. Christian Eriksen pulled one back with almost the last kick of the game, but this was City's day – yet again!

official Twitter
15

Danilo's goal rounded off a comfortable win against Bournemouth

PREMIER LEAGUE CHAMPIONS

THE MARCH OF THE CENTURIONS

MATCHDAY 19

Etihad Stadium, 23.12.17

MANCHESTER CITY 4
AFC BOURNEMOUTH 0

Agüero 27, 79, Sterling 53, Danilo 85

Another game, another flurry of milestones as City eased past Bournemouth to secure a 17th successive Premier League win. In a low key first half Sergio Agüero broke the deadlock with a diving header from Fernandinho's pass, his 100th goal at the Etihad Stadium. Raheem Sterling doubled the advantage after half-time with a first-time effort from Agüero's through ball, before the striker headed his second – and City's third – the club's 100th Premier League goal of 2017, from sub Bernardo Silva's cross. And Danilo – another replacement – finished off the rout when he coolly slotted home from Sterling's pass. It means City have gone the whole of 2017 unbeaten at home in all competitions and have become the first English team to score 100 top-flight league goals in a calendar year, since Liverpool in 1982.

MATCHDAY 20

St James' Park, 27.12.17

NEWCASTLE UNITED 0
MANCHESTER CITY 1

Sterling 31

Dominant City secured an incredible 18th successive Premier League victory to move 15 points clear at the top of the table. Raheem Sterling supplied the winner – City's 200th under Pep Guardiola – finishing Kevin De Bruyne's sublime assist for his 17th goal of a fruitful campaign. The game started with Jonjo Shelvey's shot from the kick-off towards Ederson – but after that it was virtually all one-way traffic in the other direction. City's possession was over 80 per cent for large parts of the match, with De Bruyne and Ilkay Gündogan orchestrating, and ultimately the margin of victory could have been greater but for the woodwork, which Sergio Agüero hit twice and De Bruyne once. And although Newcastle did mount a late rally, and Dwight Gayle headed wide late on, City claimed the points.

macron

Ederson came to the Blues' rescue at Selhurst Park

PREMIER LEAGUE CHAMPIONS

THE MARCH OF THE CENTURIONS

MATCHDAY 21

Selhurst Park, 31.12.17

CRYSTAL PALACE 0
MANCHESTER CITY 0

Ederson was City's hero as he saved a stoppage-time penalty to earn the Blues a hard-fought draw at Crystal Palace. City were far from their best against a spirited home side. The Eagles twice went close in the first half through Christian Benteke and Patrick van Aanholt, while City substitute Sergio Agüero cut past two challenges before sending a deflected shot beyond Wayne Hennessey and against the post. Ilkay Gündogan curled a shot a foot wide from 18 yards in the second half, while Hennessey denied Leroy Sané. Andros Townsend blazed high over the bar with the goal at his mercy in the latter stages, while at the other end Kevin De Bruyne's low shot was scrambled clear. The drama then reached fever pitch in added time as the hosts were awarded a controversial penalty for a foul on Wilfried Zaha – but Ederson beat out Luka Milivojevic's effort to earn a draw in a frantic finish.

MATCHDAY 22

Etihad Stadium, 02.01.18

MANCHESTER CITY 3
WATFORD 1

Sterling 1, Kabasele 13 (og), Agüero 63 • Gray 82

City moved 15 points clear of second-placed Manchester United with a comfortable victory over Watford. The Blues were two goals up inside the first quarter of an hour. Raheem Sterling took just 38 seconds to set City on their way from Leroy Sané cross, his 18th of the season also being the club's fastest-ever Premier League goal. John Stones should have doubled the advantage but it mattered little, as Kevin De Bruyne's cross was turned past Heurelho Gomes by Hornets defender Christian Kabasele. The Belgian playmaker slammed a free-kick against the bar as City continued to threaten, although Andre Gray twice forced Ederson into saves in an eventful first half. Sergio Agüero added a third on 63 minutes after Gomes had spilled De Bruyne's cross while Gray pulled a goal back late on. All in all, a comfortable way to start 2018!

ETIHAD
AIRWAYS
GOAL

Sergio Agüero scored a perfect hat-trick against Newcastle

PREMIER LEAGUE CHAMPIONS

THE MARCH OF THE CENTURIONS

MATCHDAY 23

Anfield, 14.01.18

LIVERPOOL 4
MANCHESTER CITY 3

Oxlade-Chamberlain 9, Firmino 59, Mané 61, Salah 68 • Sané 40, Bernardo Silva 84 Gündogan 90

A brave late fightback wasn't enough to prevent City slipping to their first Premier League defeat of the season. Leroy Sané, Bernardo Silva and Ilkay Gündogan all found the target, but a three-goal blast inside nine minutes midway through the second half secured victory for Liverpool. In a seesaw match, Sané cancelled out Alex Oxlade-Chamberlain's early strike to leave the game level at the break. But after Nicolas Otamendi had struck the bar with a superb header, quickfire goals from Roberto Firmino, Sadio Mané and, memorably, Mo Salah from 35 yards out put the hosts 4-1 up before City threatened to stage a remarkable late recovery first through sub Silva, then Gündogan. But, alas, it was not to be – the unbeaten record was over...

MATCHDAY 24

Etihad Stadium, 20.01.18

MANCHESTER CITY 3
NEWCASTLE UNITED 1

Agüero 34, 63 (pen), 83 • Murphy 67

There was no hangover from the chastening defeat on Merseyside six days earlier as City got back to winning ways, thanks to Sergio Agüero's perfect hat-trick. The Argentinian genius broke the deadlock with a glancing header from Kevin De Bruyne's pin-point cross, and it should have been more before he converted from the spot shortly after the hour-mark, making no mistake after Javier Manquillo had brought down Sterling. But Newcastle to their credit didn't fold, and four minutes later Jacob Murphy produced a cool chip over the onrushing Ederson. Both goalkeepers then took centre stage: Karl Darlow somehow pushed Sterling's close-range effort onto a post, while at the other end Ederson denied Mo Diame with a brilliant stop. Agüero completed his hat-trick late on from Leroy Sané's brilliant assist.

Bernardo Silva helps Danilo celebrate his stunning goal at Burnley

PREMIER LEAGUE CHAMPIONS

THE MARCH OF THE CENTURIONS

MATCHDAY 25

Etihad Stadium, 31.01.18

MANCHESTER CITY 3
WEST BROMWICH ALBION 0

Fernandinho 19, De Bruyne 68 Agüero 89

City moved 15 points clear of the chasing pack with a comfortable win over West Brom. On a night when new signing Aymeric Laporte made an impressive debut, the Blues controlled the game. Inevitably, Kevin De Bruyne was the architect of the opening goal as he spotted Fernandinho's run and sliced the Baggies' defence open with a pass that the Brazilian slid past Ben Foster. Albion's goal then lived a charmed life until City turned the screw and a second goal arrived midway through the second half. De Bruyne powered forward, passed to Sterling who returned the ball for the Belgian to sweep home from close range - the Blues' 100th in all competitions. Brahim Diaz and Bernardo Silva went close in the time that remained before Agüero applied the icing on the cake with a deft chip over Foster following good work by Sterling.

MATCHDAY 26

Turf Moor, 03.02.18

BURNLEY 1
MANCHESTER CITY 1

Berg Gudmundsson 82 • Danilo 22

City missed a host of opportunities and ultimately paid the price late on as Burnley claimed what had looked like an unlikely point. Danilo's first-half howitzer was scant reward as the Blues failed to kill off the hosts and a late equaliser gave the Clarets a point when, on another day, they could have been licking their wounds after a heavy loss. At a rain-soaked Turf Moor, City took the lead in spectacular fashion after 22 minutes as Danilo curled a powerful shot high and out of Nick Pope's reach. With an hour played, the only mystery was how City weren't maybe three or four clear – and judging by the various reactions of Pep Guardiola, it was a genuine concern that his players had not yet put the game beyond Burnley. The Clarets made the Blues pay when a long ball into the box was half-volleyed home by Johann Berg Gudmundsson with just eight minutes remaining.

Sergio Agüero hit four goals in an awesome display against Leicester City

PREMIER LEAGUE CHAMPIONS

THE MARCH OF THE CENTURIONS

MATCHDAY 27

Eihad Stadium, 10.02.18

MANCHESTER CITY 5
LEICESTER CITY 1

Sterling 3, Agüero 48, 53, 77, 90 • Vardy 24

A brilliant four-goal haul by Sergio Agüero steered City to a 5-1 win over Leicester at the Etihad to go 16 points clear at the top. Raheem Sterling put the Blues ahead early on, converting Kevin De Bruyne's low cross to score his 20th goal of a prolific campaign. The Foxes offered little threat until the ball fell to Jamie Vardy who skipped past two challenges before drilling a low shot past Ederson. The Blues shifted up a couple of gears after the re-start. On 49 minutes Agüero turned in De Bruyne's sumptuous low cross. A few minutes later the Argentine span and tucked home a low shot. With 13 minutes to go Agüero completed his hat-trick, intercepting Kasper Schmeichel's pass before chipping the ball back over the Dane. And in the final minute Sergio capped a memorable display with a thumping shot from 20 yards.

MATCHDAY 28

Emirates Stadium, 01.03.18

ARSENAL 0
MANCHESTER CITY 3

B. Silva 15, D. Silva 28, Sané 33

City moved 16 points clear at the top of the Premier League with their biggest away win over Arsenal since 1912. The Blues established a three-goal lead by the break after playing some scintillating football. Ederson saved a second-half penalty to compound Arsenal's miserable evening. The first-half onslaught began as Leroy Sané glided past four Arsenal players and passed to Bernardo Silva who checked inside before curling a sublime shot beyond Petr Cech. For the second goal, Sané burst down the wing before picking out Sergio Agüero whose gentle pass into David Silva's path saw the Spaniard dart in and lift the ball over Cech. And there was more to come soon after. David Silva started a move that involved Sergio Agüero and Kevin De Bruyne before Kyle Walker's cross was bundled home by Sané.

Bernardo Silva's finish was the difference in the match against Chelsea

PREMIER LEAGUE CHAMPIONS

THE MARCH OF THE CENTURIONS

MATCHDAY 29

Etihad Stadium, 04.03.18

MANCHESTER CITY 1
CHELSEA 0

B. Silva 46

City ground out a hard-fought 1-0 victory over Chelsea to move 18 points clear and confirm their status as champions-elect. Bernardo Silva sealed the win with a goal seconds after the restart in a game of few clear opportunities. The first half was low on goalmouth action until a quickly-taken free-kick by Kevin De Bruyne saw Sergio Agüero break clear and mis-hit a low shot towards the far post where Leroy Sané slid the ball home – but the assistant referee's flag was raised for offside. However, the second half was a different story with City going ahead within 35 seconds of the restart. Agüero capitalised on a mix-up in the Chelsea defence, fed the ball to the overlapping David Silva and his fine cross was met by Bernardo whose improvised finish left Thibaut Courtois floundering as the ball skipped over his head.

MATCHDAY 30

bet365 Stadium, 12.03.18

STOKE CITY 0
MANCHESTER CITY 2

Silva 10, 50

David Silva scored a goal in each half as City beat Stoke 2-0. After a stirring pre-match rendition of Tom Jones' 'Delilah', the home crowd were clearly in the mood to be the Potters' twelfth man, but there have been plenty of times when a twelfth, thirteenth or even fourteenth man wouldn't have beaten this City team. And it took less than 10 minutes for the Blues to demonstrate their class. Fernandinho played a ball to Gabriel Jesus' feet and the Brazilian striker spotted Raheem Sterling's run, fed him the ball and Sterling's low cross was stroked home with power by David Silva. City doubled the lead within five minutes of the restart with another sublime goal that again involved Fernandinho and Jesus with the latter playing an improvised one-two with the majestic Silva who scored his second of the night as he expertly volleyed home.

Fan passion on display on derby day

PREMIER LEAGUE CHAMPIONS

THE MARCH OF THE CENTURIONS

MATCHDAY 31

Goodison Park, 31.03.18

EVERTON 1
MANCHESTER CITY 3

Bolasie 63 • Sané 4, Jesus 12, Sterling 37

City demonstrated how far they've come in a season by strolling to victory against Everton at Goodison Park. This fixture last season saw the Blues suffer a demoralising 4-0 defeat but it took Pep Guardiola's men only four minutes to show how much they've improved since. David Silva got to the byline and hooked the ball back for Leroy Sané to slam the ball in on the volley. It was 2-0 soon after as assist-king Kevin De Bruyne delivered the perfect cross for Gabriel Jesus, who headed past Jordan Pickford. The third goal duly arrived after 37 minutes. David Silva was sent through down the left and crossed for Sterling to finish at the back post. City's dominance continued after the break - despite Bolasie's well-struck goal just after the hour - and the Blues secured Guardiola's first victory over the Toffees.

MATCHDAY 32

Etihad Stadium, 07.04.18

MANCHESTER CITY 2
MANCHESTER UNITED 3

Kompany 25, Gündogan 30 • Pogba 53, 55, Smalling 69

City threw a two-goal first-half lead away to lose 3-2 to United in a dramatic, and ultimately crushing, Manchester derby. At half-time it seemed impossible to lose a game that City were in total control of. Pep Guardiola's men struck first as Vincent Kompany rose highest to thump a header in from Leroy Sane's corner. The second arrived on the half-hour mark as Ilkay Gündogan span off his marker and toe-poked home. In the 15 first-half minutes that remained, the Blues were at their sublime best and Raheem Sterling could have helped himself to a hat-trick. But there was to be a huge twist in the tale after the break. Paul Pogba scored twice in three minutes and the turnaround was complete when an Alexis Sanchez cross from a free-kick was volleyed in by Chris Smalling. Title celebrations would have to wait a little longer.

Fabian Delph lets out a roar of delight after a big win at Wembley

PREMIER LEAGUE CHAMPIONS

THE MARCH OF THE CENTURIONS

MATCHDAY 33

Wembley Stadium, 14.04.18

TOTTENHAM HOTSPUR 1
MANCHESTER CITY 3

Eriksen 42 • Jesus 22, Gündogan 25 (pen), Sterling 72

Spurs were swept aside 3-1 with much of the hard work done in a devastating first half-hour. If City were hurting from defeats to United and Liverpool, it didn't show in the opening moments of this game at Wembley that saw them take control thanks to a cool finish from Gabriel Jesus and a calmly-taken penalty by Ilkay Gündogan, after Raheem Sterling had been fouled by Spurs keeper Hugo Lloris. These goals came after Leroy Sané had already smacked a volley against the post. Spurs improved before the break and pulled a fortuitous goal back as Aymeric Laporte's attempted clearance cannoned off the shins of Christian Eriksen and into the net. City confirmed the three points on 72 minutes when Lloris kept out Jesus' shot, but Sterling was on hand to hammer in the rebound from four yards.

MATCHDAY 34

Etihad Stadium, 22.04.18

MANCHESTER CITY 5
SWANSEA CITY 0

Silva 12, Sterling 16, De Bruyne 54, Bernardo Silva 64, Jesus 88

City walked out to a guard of honour for their match against Swansea, knowing they had been confirmed as champions between matches – and they proceeded to produce a performance befitting of the best team in the land. The Blues were merciless from the start and David Silva started the rout, volleying in from the left before Fabian Delph's low cross was converted by Raheem Sterling to make it 2-0. The pick of the bunch came from Kevin De Bruyne who rocketed in from outside the box after the break. Just past the hour it was 4-0 as Gabriel Jesus' penalty was tipped onto the post, and Bernardo Silva reacted first to blast home. Gabriel Jesus put the icing on the cake with a clever header from Yaya Toure's exquisite chip. Not a bad way to celebrate the title!

The London Stadium saw another City goal rush, with Leroy Sané scoring the opener

PREMIER LEAGUE CHAMPIONS

THE MARCH OF THE CENTURIONS

MATCHDAY 35

London Stadium, 29.04.18

WEST HAM UNITED 1
MANCHESTER CITY 4

Cresswell 42 • Sané 13, Zabaleta (og), Jesus 53, Fernandinho 64

City chalked up their 30th Premier League win of the season with a 4-1 victory at the London Stadium. The four goals brought Pep Guardiola's men to 102 for the season, just one short of Chelsea's Premier League best. Leroy Sané broke the deadlock after 13 minutes and the lead doubled when Declan Rice failed to deal with Kevin De Bruyne's low cross and the defender's attempted clearance brushed off Pablo Zabaleta and trickled in. Aaron Cresswell halved the arrears with a fine free-kick but City stepped up a gear after the restart. Gabriel Jesus took Raheem Sterling's return ball, skipped past Zabaleta and finished past Adrian. Then Fernandinho won the ball high up the field and continued his run to take Sterling's pass and finish from 12 yards.

MATCHDAY 36

Etihad Stadium, 06.05.18

MANCHESTER CITY 0
HUDDERSFIELD TOWN 0

City were held to a goalless draw by Huddersfield Town who claimed an unlikely point and ended up being the first Premier League side to stop City scoring at the Etihad all season. With the flags flying, the sun-drenched crowd looked spectacular and ready to party ahead of kick-off. But what followed was a disjointed game and the Blues below their sparkling best. There were few opportunities for the champions other than a low effort from David Silva and a Kevin De Bruyne shot that whistled the wrong side of the post. As the clock ticked down and the visitors edged nearer a priceless point, sub Bernardo Silva volleyed a low shot inches past Jonas Lossl's left-hand post. In the dying seconds, the Terriers twice broke forward and but for some desperate defending, could have taken all three points. At least there was the Premier League trophy lift to end the afternoon!

Danilo takes the acclaim after scoring in the final home game of the season, against Brighton

MATCHDAY 37

Etihad Stadium, 09.05.18

MANCHESTER CITY 3
BRIGHTON & HOVE ALBION 1

Danilo 16, Bernardo Silva 34, Fernandinho 72 • Ulloa 20

City set three new Premier League records as Yaya Toure signed off in style with a 3-1 win over Brighton. The Blues marked the Ivorian's farewell Etihad appearance by breaking the Premier League record for most wins, most goals and most points in a season. The game began with cheers for every touch Yaya made and ended with him almost finding the net before being taken off to a huge ovation. In between times City had a game to win, and they opened the scoring when Leroy Sané fed through a perfect ball for Danilo to finish. After a Brighton equaliser through a Leonardo Ulloa header, the Blues regained the lead on 34 minutes as Sané's low cross was drilled home by Bernardo. The champions put the game to bed on 72 minutes when Sané completed a hat-trick of assists as he picked out Fernandinho who drilled home a low shot.

MATCHDAY 38

St Mary's Stadium, 13.05.18

SOUTHAMPTON 0
MANCHESTER CITY 1

Gabriel Jesus 90+3

Gabriel Jesus scored a dramatic added-time winner to take City to the magical 100-point mark. The 1-0 win over Southampton was the perfect end to a perfect season. The sell-out crowd were in the mood for a party with safety almost assured for the Saints. The hosts started well and could have been ahead on eight minutes when Wesley Hoedt headed a corner against the crossbar. City shifted up a gear after the break and the Blues came agonisingly close twice within the space of a minute as first Raheem Sterling rattled the post and then John Stones saw a header tipped over by Alex McCarthy. Dusan Tadic should have scored on 77 minutes but Fernandinho cleared his shot off the line. Then, deep in added time, Gabriel Jesus raced on to a Kevin De Bruyne pass to lob the ball over McCarthy for a dramatic end to a wonderful campaign.

CELEBRATING CENTURIONS

The hard work was done. Now it was time to claim the gleaming prize and show it to the blue masses – both at the Etihad Stadium and on the streets of Manchester

100
POINTS
MANCHESTER CITY
PREMIER LEAGUE CHAMPIONS
CARABAO CUP WINNERS
/18
3
2
1

ETIHAD
AIRWAYS
Premier League
NEXEN TIRE

ETIHAD
AIRWAYS
Premier League
NEXEN
TIRE

Premier League
ETIHAD AIRWAYS

Premier League

CHAMPIONS
18
NEXEN TIRE

Premier League

Premier League

Premier League
Premier League
Premier League
Premier League
MANCHESTER
CITY

CHAMPIONS
18
25

Premier League

Premier League
Premier League
Premier League
Premier League
MANCHESTER CITY
ONLY

CHAMPIONS 2017/18

CHAMPIONS 2017/18

Premier League
GEORGE'S

ENERGY

Premier League
Premier League
Premier League
Premier League
Premier League
Premier League

Thank you
YAYA
ONLY
CITY
CHAMPIONS

Premier League
MANCHESTER CITY

42

YAYA TOURE

Though Yaya Toure became a more peripheral figure on matchdays throughout the 2017/18 season, his popularity never waned during what would be his final campaign with City.

The Ivorian, surely one of the best players to ever represent the Club, spent much of his eighth season on the bench and so wasn't able to make the kind of telling contributions he had in the past, but he still picked up two more winner's medals to make it a total of eight in eight years. City had failed to win any silverware for 35 years before Yaya signed and it's no coincidence that things started to happen after his arrival.

Yaya was restricted to just 10 appearances in the Premier League but added a further seven in cup competitions and he was given an emotional send-off in his final game for the Blues as he captained the team against Brighton and Hove Albion.

City won the game 3-1, but the goal the City fans craved – a Yaya special – never came.

Despite his lack of minutes, he still managed to provide two assists and will be forever remembered as a true Manchester City legend.

PEP SAYS...

"Yaya Toure came here when this idea for the Club started, and what we are in this moment is thanks to what this guy has done. We cannot forget the period from Roberto Mancini, and especially Manuel Pellegrini. He has been a key, key player for this Club."

STATS...

Not as telling a contribution as he would have wanted in his final campaign for the Blues, but Yaya still contributed whenever he came on with his usual excellent passing range and vision. Two assists and just one full Premier League appearance tells its own story.

YAYA TOURE	
Position:	Midfielder
Date of birth:	13 May 1983
Place of birth:	Bouake, Ivory Coast
2017/2018	(all competitions)
Appearances	17
Goals	0
Assists	2

STADIUM
Premier League
MANCHESTER
CITY
Premier League
18

18

FABIAN DELPH

Fabian Delph enjoyed the best season of his career in 2017/18.

It began on the bench, with Delph perhaps feeling he would have to be patient for opportunities to arise, but in the game against Crystal Palace where Benjamin Mendy suffered a cruciate ligament injury, his season completely changed.

Delph had trained as a left-back occasionally and though Danilo was capable of filling in there if needed, it was the England midfielder who grasped the opportunity.

In fact, it was hard not to believe Delph had always played in defence, given the calibre of his displays and the former Aston Villa and Leeds star proved a more than competent deputy for Mendy.

Efficient and tidy with the occasional biting tackle, Delph kept things simple at the back and would look to win possession and then play the ball to a team-mate. It's fair to say that no wide player got the better of Delph all season and he featured in 22 league games and 29 in all competitions.

So impressive was Delph that he won a place in the England World Cup squad, despite not playing for his country since 2016.

It was a surprise for many, but not for City fans who saw Delph as something of an unsung hero.

macron

CITYZENS
ETIHAD
CAMPU
MANCHESTER
CITY

NEXEN TIRE
ETIHAD
AIRWAYS

AIA
20
18

“WE’RE A POWERFUL FORCE AT THE MINUTE AND LONG MAY IT CONTINUE.”

ETIHAD
AIRWAYS
ETIHAD
AIRWAYS

"He is a player who can play in different positions, he helps us to play good football, to be better, to give an extra pass. And he has a good heart, he is a fantastic person. I think he is a guy for the group. Last season, he didn't play but he always helped the team, he was always there."

STATS...

Delph has proved to be one of the most consistent defenders in the Premier League based on his 22 games. With a 74% tackle success rate, 30 interceptions and 114 duels won, it's not hard to understand why he became such an important member of the squad.

FABIAN DELPH	
Position:	Midfielder
Date of birth:	21 November 1989
Place of birth:	Bradford, England
2017/2018	(all competitions)
Appearances	29
Goals	1
Assists	2

Premier League

10

SERGIO AGÜERO

Given Sergio Agüero missed the best part of three months with injury, his 2017/18 stats are nothing short of incredible.

The Argentina star scored 30 goals from 32 starts in what was a rollercoaster of a season of ups and downs.

The ups were when he played, the downs were the injury sustained in a car crash and the knee issue that eventually needed surgery that had been plaguing him for several years.

Sergio had several blistering bursts of goal-scoring form during the campaign including 15 goals between January and February when he helped himself to a couple of hat-tricks – he would score three in total – as he chased down several Club records.

He levelled with Eric Brook's 79-year tally of 177 goals with a penalty against Burnley in October and then became the Blues' all-time record scorer with a goal away to Napoli.

His knee problem meant his last game of yet another prolific campaign was in mid-April, leaving him agonisingly on 199 goals in all competitions. He ended the season with 30 goals from 39 appearances in all competitions and given he could have played in a further 18 matches had he been selected/fit for all games and Kun might have topped the 40-goal mark or higher – who knows?

Yet for all the 'could have beens', he still made a huge contribution to the Blues' season, ending top scorer yet again and writing more chapters into his incredible career with City.

Agüero is undoubtedly the best striker the Blues have ever had and one of – if not the – best in the world.

ETIHAD
AIRWAYS

ETIHAD
AIRWAYS

ETIHAD
AIRWAYS
SAN
ISSA

“IT’S BEEN A PLEASURE TO PLAY WITH THIS TEAM AND BE PART OF EVERYTHING WE’VE ACHIEVED. WE HAVE SCORED GREAT GOALS, PLAYED FANTASTIC FOOTBALL AND LEARNED TOGETHER UNDER PEP.”

ETIHAD
AIRWAYS
10

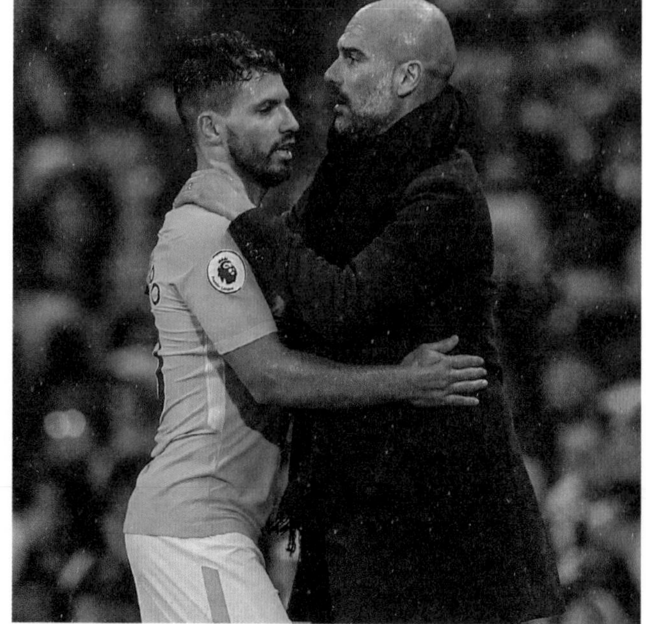

PEP SAYS...

"I'm so demanding with him because I always think he can do better. It is not for any other reason than to help him. We are so delighted with what he has done over the last two seasons, with the goals he has scored and the way he has tried to help us with and without the ball. 199 goals? Wow! I am delighted with the goals he has scored so far."

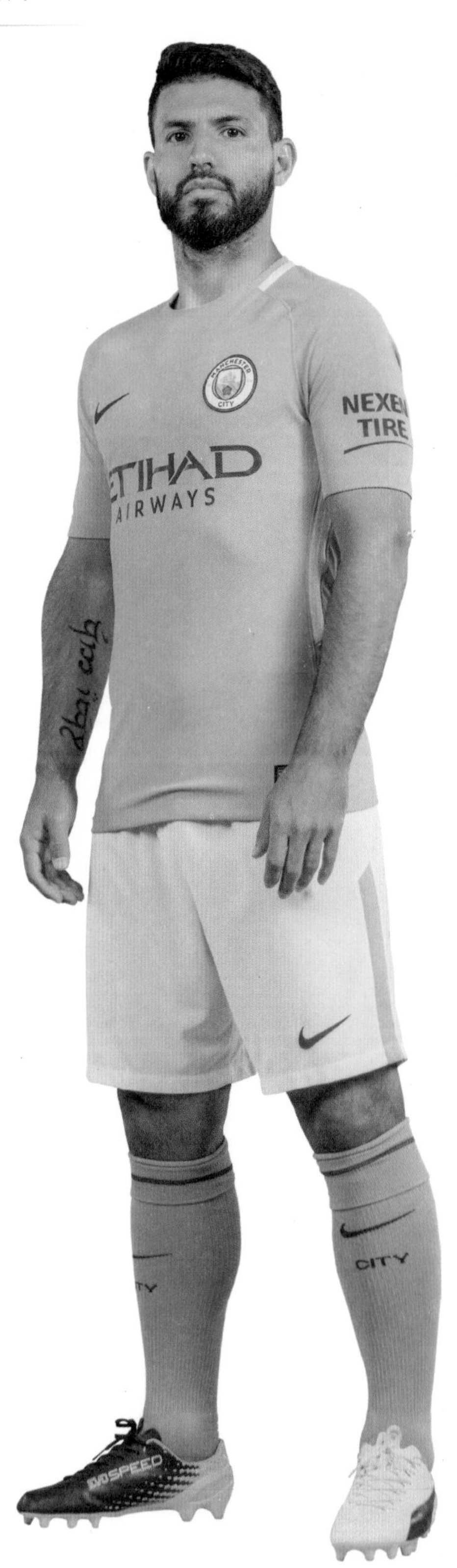

STATS...

Sergio enhanced his reputation yet further in 2017/18 and playing under Pep Guardiola has clearly added to his all-round game. He made six assists for his team-mates and created a further 10 'big chances' as well as striking the woodwork three times. His 30 goals came from just 32 starts – phenomenal.

SERGIO AGÜERO	
Position:	Striker
Date of birth:	02 June 1988
Place of birth:	Buenos Aires, Argentina
2017/2018	(all competitions)
Appearances	39
Goals	30
Assists	6

Premier League
Premier League

JOHN STONES

As City powered through the first three months of the season, there probably wasn't a better defender in the Premier League than John Stones, who missed just one of the first 12 games.

He added goals to his game, too, and at one stage was among the leading scorers in the Champions League with three in four games!

The young England star was superb and looked every inch the player he had been touted to be for the past few years – then, a hamstring injury at Leicester stopped him in his tracks and he was sidelined for six weeks.

Though he was back for January, Stones would struggle with various knocks for the remainder of the campaign, but he'd more than played his part in getting City on the launchpad to an incredible season.

Stones is the archetypal Guardiola player – comfortable on the ball, technically excellent and quick. He is happy to receive the ball from the goalkeeper and play under pressure and the former Everton and Barnsley defender is only going to get better.

By the end of his second season at the Etihad, Stones had played 29 games in all competitions and realised a boyhood dream by becoming a Premier League champion.

He will look to start the 2018/19 campaign in the same manner he began the 2017/18 and kick on again as City look to retain the title and challenge strongly in the Champions League.

There is, without doubt, much more to come from John Stones.

ETIHAD
AIRWAYS

ETIHAD
AIRWAYS

AIA

CITYZENS

ETIHAD

"ME AND KYLE WALKER WERE SAYING THAT THIS IS WHY WE CAME HERE. WE JUST NEVER KNEW WHAT IT WOULD FEEL LIKE TO LIFT THE PREMIER LEAGUE TROPHY. IT LITERALLY IS JUST A DREAM COME TRUE."

ETIHAD
AIRWAYS
ETIHAD
AIRWAYS
DANILO
3
CITY
ETIHAD
AIRWAYS

PEP SAYS...

"He is a young player, an international English player. He's a huge part of the reason why we won the title. I don't know how long I will be here in Manchester, but as long as I'm here, John Stones will be with us."

STATS...

Stones began the campaign without putting a foot wrong – strong, assured and effective, he started 18 of the Blues' first 20 games, scoring three goals – and City won 19 of those matches. Impressive stuff.

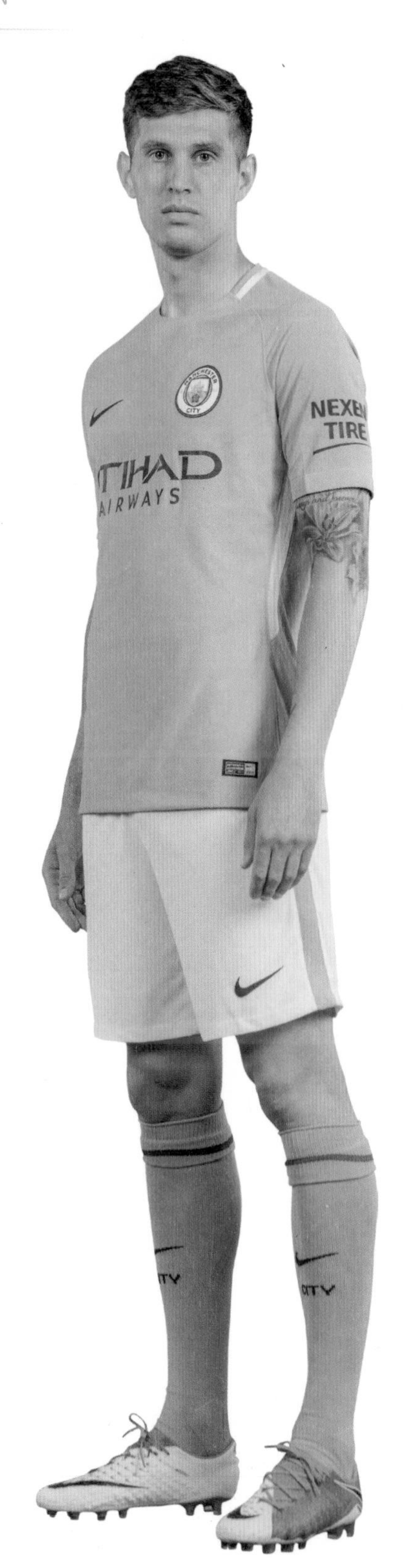

JOHN STONES	
Position:	Defender
Date of birth:	28 May 1994
Place of birth:	Barnsley, England
2017/2018	(all competitions)
Appearances	29
Goals	3
Assists	0

Premier League
League
Premier League
Premier League
Premier League

31

EDERSON MORAES

To say Ederson hit the ground running in his first season with City is an understatement. Rarely, if ever, has a goalkeeper become such an integral member of a team so quickly and with such excellence.

His distribution is, perhaps, the best in the world and he is equally comfortable with the ball at his feet as he is with it in his hands.

Recruiting Ederson was a masterstroke by City. On paper, he didn't have that much experience, was young and was not an established international. He'd barely had 18 months as Benfica's first-choice keeper, but he'd done enough to convince the Blues that he was the perfect custodian to lead from the back, so to speak.

And not only was he a youngster living thousands of miles from Brazil, he was coming to a new league, new country and effectively taking over from the experienced Claudio Bravo.

On his debut away to Brighton, it quickly became apparent that he was different from any goalkeeper City had employed before.

Calmness personified on the ball, he was soon spraying 60-yard balls upfield to perfection but was solid and dependable whenever called upon to make a save. In fact, it's hard to find any chinks in his armour.

He quickly became a cult figure among the City fans with that bond strengthened early as he bravely headed clear a ball and was caught by a high Sadio Mane boot. The Liverpool forward was dismissed and the Blues went on to win 5-0, though Ederson was left with a nasty facial gash and stretchered off.

He was back for the next game and would play 45 times in his debut campaign and ended with 16 clean sheets in the Premier League, just two shy of Golden Glove winner David De Gea.

A remarkable campaign for a hugely talented keeper.

AIRWAYS

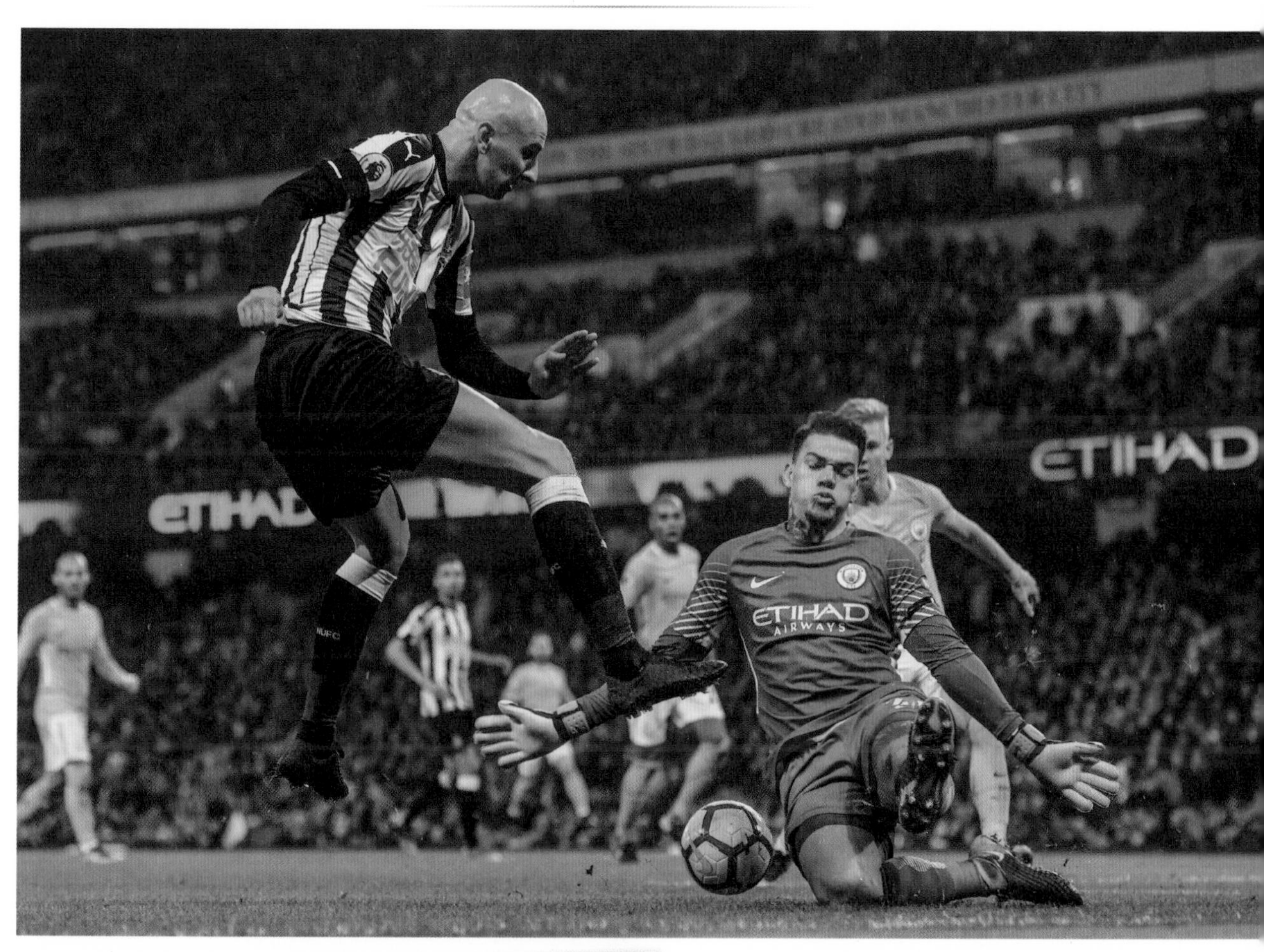
ETIHAD
ETIHAD
ETIHAD
AIRWAYS

"THE CLUB IS HAPPY WITH MY WORK, THEY TRUST ME, AND I HOPE TO MEET THEIR EXPECTATIONS ON THE PITCH AND BRING A LOT OF JOY TO THE FANS."

CITYZENS

PEP SAYS...

"He is one of the top keepers. With his age and his desire to improve he will become an extraordinary goalkeeper. The most important thing is he is so calm. When he concedes a goal he is quiet and when he makes an extraordinary save he is quiet. His reaction is the same. He is so stable."

STATS...

Ederson played all but the last two Premier League games for City and was the Champions League goalkeeper with Claudio Bravo preferred for the domestic cup competitions. His 16 clean sheets were the second best in the division, but what the stats won't show is the amount of times he started moves from the back with incisive passes that eventually led to goals.

EDERSON MORAES	
Position:	Goalkeeper
Date of birth:	17 August 1993
Place of birth:	Osasco, Brazil
2017/2018	(all competitions)
Appearances	45
Goals	0
Assists	0

Carabao ENERGY DRINK
Carabao ENERGY DRINK
Premier League
Premier League
Premier League

30

NICOLAS OTAMENDI

Throughout the various central defensive partnerships City employed during the season, Nicolas Otamendi was the one constant.

The Argentine clocked up 46 appearances in all competitions and had his best campaign yet for the Blues.

No defender in the Premier League completed more passes than the man nicknamed 'The General' and his all-round game has moved to another level under Pep Guardiola.

He has become a crucial part of the way City play, with his distribution key to getting the ball forward from the back and it's no coincidence that his passes for the season are double that of two years ago.

Otamendi made a superb start to the season, adding goals to his passing and defending and he had bagged five goals in his first 20 games – a fantastic return for a defender.

His most memorable effort was the acrobatic winner he scored at Old Trafford to secure a 2-1 win over Manchester United in December.

It's all the more impressive because of the number of partners he had during the campaign with Vincent Kompany, John Stones and Aymeric Laporte all sharing the duties.

Aged 30, Otamendi is at the peak of his game and there is much the likes of Stones and Laporte can learn from this defensive warrior and seasoned international.

The Club ensured he will remain a City player for many years to come after he signed a contract extension until 2022 earlier this year.

A defensive lynchpin who brings so much to the team, Otamendi is likely to remain a key member of City's team for the foreseeable future.

ETIHAD
AIRWAYS

OPE

ETIHAD
AIRWAYS

"MY ONLY AIM IS TO HELP THE TEAM AND GIVE ALL I CAN FOR THIS CLUB. I AM LEARNING EVERY DAY UNDER PEP AND ENJOYING MY FOOTBALL AND I FEEL I CAN STILL IMPROVE AS A PLAYER."

OTAMENDI
30
betsafe
BET IN
dafabet
NEXEN TIRE

PEP SAYS...

"Without Nico, it would not be possible, what we have done. Everyone speaks about players such as Raheem, like David, like Kevin, like Sergio, and they deserve it, but if I would like to point to a player who deserves full respect for what they have done until now, it's Nico. Nico has been amazing."

STATS...

Otamendi topped the passing list of City players in 2017/18, pipping team-mate Fernandinho by 99! He was rested for the last two games of the campaign or else he would have topped the Premier League list as well, averaging 90 passes per game. Aside from his five goals, he also hit the woodwork twice, denying him a career best tally in the process.

NICOLAS OTAMENDI	
Position:	Defender
Date of birth:	12 February 1988
Place of birth:	Buenos Aires, Argentina
2017/2018	(all competitions)
Appearances	46
Goals	5
Assists	0

2017/18

25

FERNANDINHO

Fernandinho enjoyed, if anything, his best season yet in 2017/18 – and that's quite a statement given what has gone before.

The unflappable Brazilian is at the centre of everything City do and was magnificent throughout this record-breaking campaign.

Always available to receive the ball from Ederson or any defender under pressure, Fernandinho occupies the most important cog in the Pep Guardiola system.

In a side that refuses to panic or play the ball long, it is Fernandinho who starts everything.

There can be few more effective or classy holding midfielders than the Brazilian who has both silk and steel in his locker.

He not only starts attacks, he breaks up opposition attacks and gets the ball rolling again and he is a player Guardiola places enormous responsibility on.

His performances in key games sometimes went under the radar – he's not a player who seeks the limelight – he just gets on with his job and does what he does extremely well.

He also added five goals throughout the campaign and assisted three more for his team-mates, missing only four Premier League games all season, two of which were due to suspension.

His typically Brazilian 25-yard thunderbolt against Stoke City was voted Goal of the Season by City fans, too.

A class act who had a fantastic campaign.

25
CITYZENS
MANCHESTER
CITY
25

MANCHESTER
CITY
AIRWAYS

MAN

ETIHAD
AIRWAYS
NEXEN
TIRE
25
33

25
CITYZENS

TIHAD
25

“IT’S BEEN FIVE YEARS AND I’VE MANAGED TO KEEP PLAYING FOR MANCHESTER CITY REGULARLY - PLAYING A LOT AND WINNING TITLES. ALL OF THIS ALLOWED ME TO REACH MY GOAL, WHICH IS TO PLAY FOR THE BRAZILIAN NATIONAL TEAM.”

Premier League
ETIHAD AIRWAYS
NEXEN TIRE

PEP SAYS...

"I think Fernandinho can play in 10 different positions, because he has the quality to play wherever."

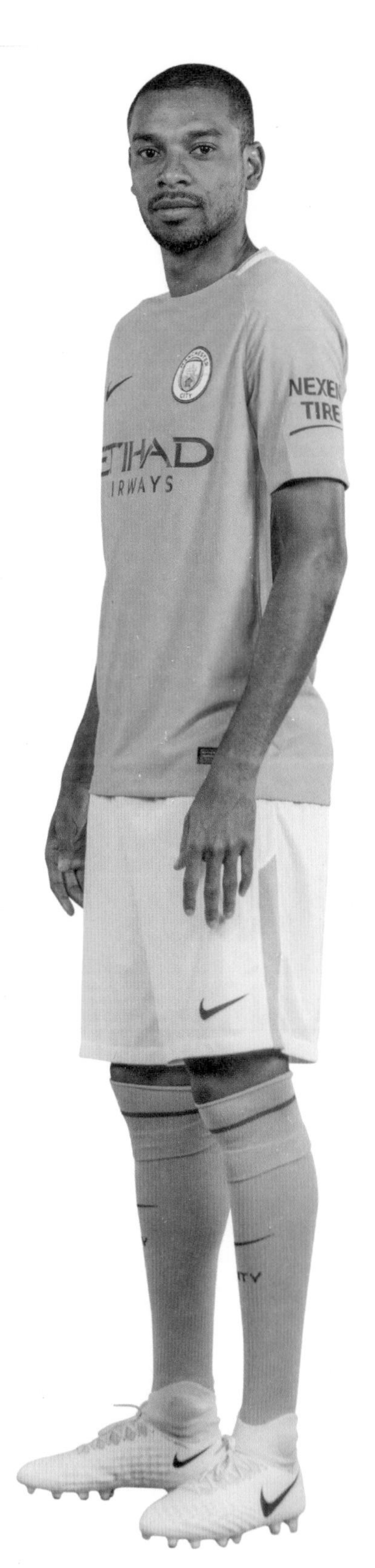

STATS...

Fernandinho came close to topping the Premier League most completed passes list for 2017/18 with just 25 shy of 3,000. He contributed in every area of the pitch – goals, assists, through-balls, tackles, recoveries – and played 48 games in all competitions.

FERNANDINHO	
Position:	Midfielder
Date of birth:	04 May 1985
Place of birth:	Londrina, Brazil
2017/2018	(all competitions)
Appearances	48
Goals	5
Assists	3

ENERGY DRINK
DRINK
DRINK
ENERGY
ENERGY DRINK

22

BENJAMIN MENDY

Touted as one of Europe's most exciting full-backs, Benjamin Mendy had posted his CV during City's Champions League matches against AS Monaco the previous season.

Powerful, quick and an attacking force down the left flank, Mendy was brought in to replace Aleksandar Kolarov and Gael Clichy who both left the Blues in the summer of 2017.

An almost unstoppable force when in full flight, he quickly added a new dimension down the left for City and was perhaps the final piece of the puzzle for Guardiola's attack-minded side.

Yet in only his fifth appearance an attempted tackle left him in agony having damaged his cruciate ligament.

The prognosis was not good, and Mendy was ruled out for up to six months.

City fans had seen enough to know his absence would be a big loss, but throughout his recovery Mendy kept a high profile on social media, coining the phrase 'shark team' and gaining a huge cult following as a result.

After Raheem Sterling's last-gasp winner at home to Southampton, he hopped down the touchline to join the celebrations, lost in the moment barely eight weeks after his operation!

He fought hard to get back as quickly as possible and, needing to prove his fitness ahead of France's World Cup squad selection, he returned against Swansea in late April to a hero's reception.

Mendy did enough to win selection for his country, an indication of how highly Les Bleus rate the powerhouse defender and he is likely to be a huge asset for City next season.

PEP SAYS...

"It's a joy to train with him."

STATS...

The fact Mendy has managed 39 crosses in just seven games underlines what an attacking tour de force he is. His 80% success rate at tackles proves he is a defender first and foremost, but expect his assists to be in double figures next season.

BENJAMIN MENDY	
Position:	Defender
Date of birth:	17 July 1994
Place of birth:	Longjumeau, France
2017/2018	(all competitions)
Appearances	7
Goals	0
Assists	1

NEXEN
TIRE

14

AYMERIC LAPORTE

It's never easy joining a club midway through the season, particularly when you're joining the runaway leaders of one of the toughest leagues in the world.

As ever, Pep Guardiola got things spot on, blooding the youngster here and there as he found his feet in the Premier League.

Laporte was given time to adapt before being given a run of games that allowed him to settle in and adjust to the pace and power of English football.

Laporte arrived from Athletic Bilbao where he'd established himself as one of Europe's most promising defenders.

A calm, ball-playing centre-back capable of filling in at left-back, Laporte marked his debut with a 60-yard raking pass to the feet of a team-mate to underline his technical ability was on point.

Laporte oozes class, is comfortable in possession and looks an excellent addition to the Blues' squad.

He is strong, too, more than holding his own in the games he's played so far and in future seasons the French-born defender could be the perfect partner for John Stones.

With half a season now under his belt, expect Laporte to hit the ground running in the 2018/19 season and feature regularly in the starting XI.

An impressive start to life with the Blues and there's much more to come from the youngster.

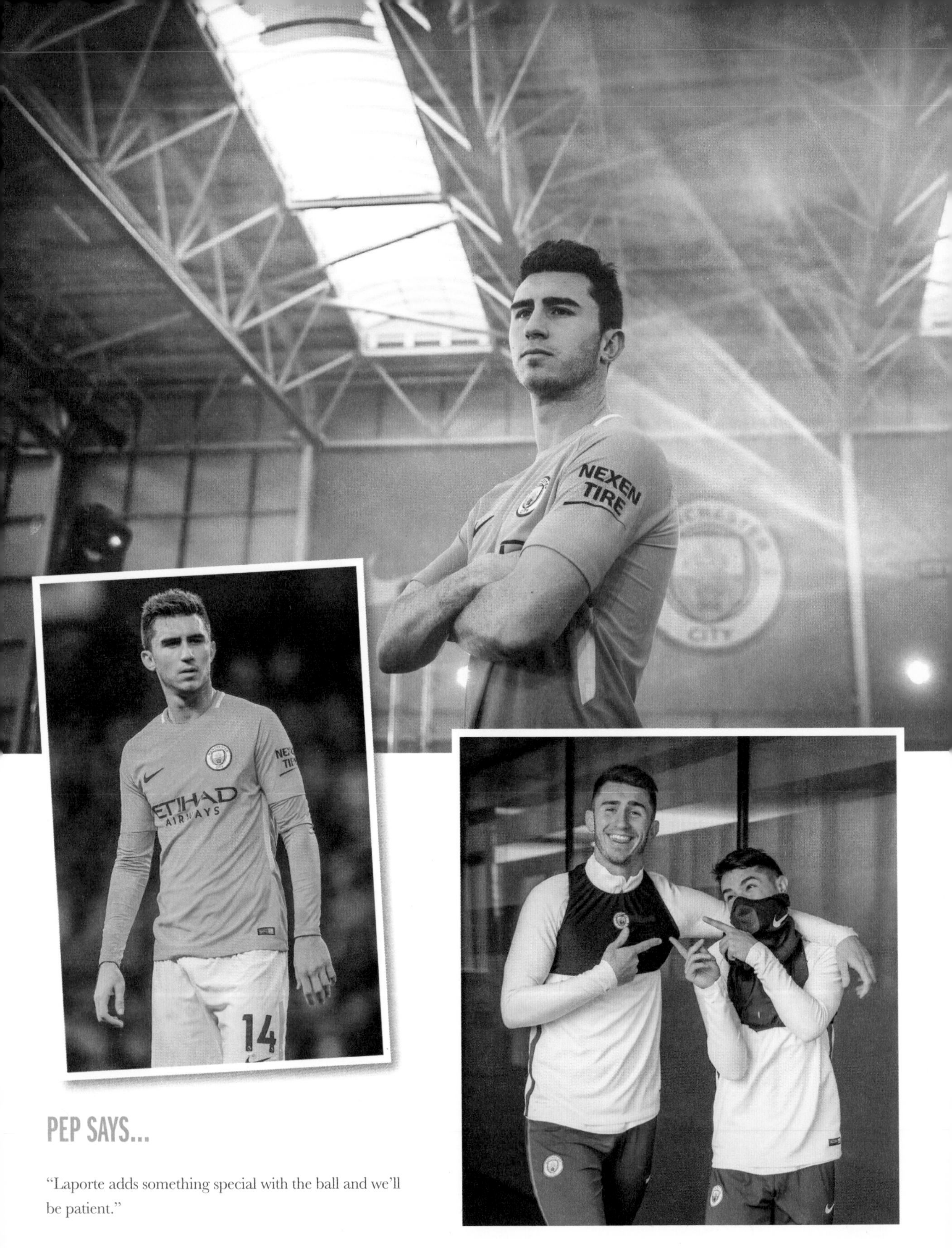

PEP SAYS...

"Laporte adds something special with the ball and we'll be patient."

STATS...

With an 88% tackle success from his nine Premier League games and an average of 90 passes per game, Laporte comfortably mixes silk and steel. Add 42 accurate long balls and it's not hard to see why City were so keen to bring him to the club.

AYMERIC LAPORTE	
Position:	Defender
Date of birth:	17 May 1994
Place of birth:	Agen, France
2017/2018	(all competitions)
Appearances	13
Goals	0
Assists	0

ETIHAD
AIRWAYS
20

20

BERNARDO SILVA

Watching Bernardo Silva blossom over the season was one of the many team highlights during the 2017/18 campaign.

The diminutive playmaker needed to be patient and wait for his opportunities as Pep Guardiola eased the former Monaco star in gently, with cameos off the bench here and there.

Gradually, Bernardo started to show the kind of form that had convinced the Blues to sign him and he would end the campaign with impressive figures.

With superb technique and the deftest of touches, Bernardo would more often than not play on the right flank and he was one of the few players to feature regularly in all competitions.

The quandary for the City boss is where the Portuguese star is best utilised – he seems a natural No.10, but with David Silva and Kevin De Bruyne currently occupying those more central attacking roles, it may be a position he gently slots into over the coming years.

What is certain is that Bernardo is going to be one of the Premier League's most exciting talents and the 2018/19 season will be fascinating because he is going to get better and better.

By the end of the remarkable title-winning campaign, Bernardo had made more appearances than any other City player with 53 in total – a measure perhaps of how highly his manager rates him.

All in all, an impressive first year in English football and a player the City fans love to watch.

20
CITYZENS
20

20
8

MANCHESTER
CITY

ETIHAD
AIRWAYS

NEXEN
TIRE

"OF COURSE, I WANT TO GET EVEN BETTER, I WILL WORK AS HARD AS I CAN TO BE ABLE TO HELP THE TEAM EVEN MORE. I'M SETTLED HERE AND I FEEL BETTER AND BETTER EVERY DAY."

CITYZENS
S FROM £359
ETIHAD
ETIHAD STADIUM

PEP SAYS...

"He has an amazing quality. He connects perfectly with the way we want to play in this team. As a person, I always enjoy working with good people and he's one of them. He has amazing relations with his team-mates, coaches, everyone. It is difficult to find anyone better in that than Bernardo Silva."

STATS...

Bernardo clocked up 53 games in all competitions and scored nine goals – including a superb effort away to Cardiff that was wrongly ruled out. He made four Premier League assists but expect that to double or even treble next season.

BERNARDO SILVA	
Position:	Attacking midfielder
Date of birth:	08 January 1986
Place of birth:	Lisbon, Portugal
2017/2018	(all competitions)
Appearances	53
Goals	9
Assists	4

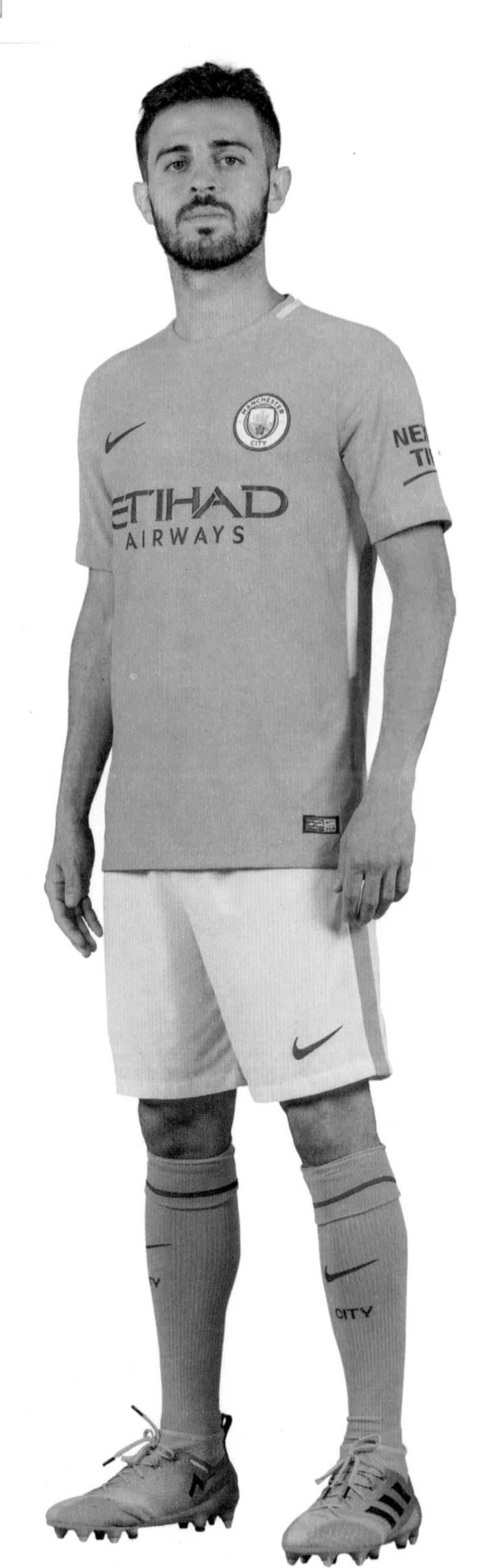

ONLY

19

LEROY SANÉ

Exciting, thrilling, devastating... the superlatives were flowing during Leroy Sané's second season with City and they're likely to continue to flow for many seasons to come.

When the Blues signed the teenage German winger from Schalke, it's fair to say that he hadn't really been on the radar of many fans in English football – but that changed after his first season at the Etihad.

His second saw Sané shift up another gear.

Blessed with devastating pace, power and athleticism, Sané has the ability to destroy defences single-handedly and there were several occasions during the 2017/18 season when he did exactly that.

Of his many excellent displays, the away trip to Arsenal saw the Germany international tear the Gunners apart as City raced into a 3-0 lead with barely half an hour played.

Of course, that was just one of the many breath-taking performances he made during a campaign that saw him become the first City player to be voted the PFA Young Player of the Year since 1976.

His stats merely scratch the surface of his second campaign in sky blue where he was pipped at the post for most Premier League assists by team-mate Kevin De Bruyne with almost the last meaningful pass of the season. He also weighed in with 14 goals in all competitions and forged a wing partnership with Raheem Sterling that must give Premier League full-backs nightmares.

Still only 22 going into the 2018/19 campaign, he is undoubtedly one of the most exciting talents in world football.

ETIHAD
AIRWAYS
19

ETIHAD

"ONE OF THE REASONS I DECIDED TO JOIN CITY WAS PEP GUARDIOLA. I KNOW I WILL LEARN A LOT UNDER HIM AND NOW I CAN TAKE THE NEXT STEP. PEP WORKS REALLY WELL WITH YOUNG PLAYERS. I THINK HE CAN MAKE ME A MORE COMPLETE PLAYER."

19
23

PEP SAYS...

"The most important thing for Leroy is consistency during the games. One guy or two guys can play good for a short period, but he's been good during a long period, excellent. His consistency was the most valuable thing. His quality speaks for itself."

STATS...

Leroy made 49 appearances in all competitions for the Centurions, chipping in with 15 Premier League assists and 14 goals in total. He made 32 league appearances, giving him an average close to one assist every other game and a goal every three matches. Not bad at all!

LEROY SANÉ	
Position:	Attacking Midfielder
Date of birth:	11 January 1994
Place of birth:	Essen, Germany
2017/2018	(all competitions)
Appearances	49
Goals	14
Assists	15

CLAUDIO BRAVO	
Position:	Goalkeeper
Date of birth:	13 April 1986
Place of birth:	Viluco, Chile
2017/2018	(all competitions)
Appearances	13
Goals	0
Assists	0

CLAUDIO BRAVO

Though Claudio Bravo assumed the role of City's back-up keeper during the 2017/18 campaign, the Chilean still clocked up 13 appearances overall.

His contribution came mainly in domestic cup competitions, with just three Premier League appearances – one of which was off the bench.

Yet Bravo played his part to the full as the Blues landed the first piece of silverware of the campaign.

It was Bravo's heroics in the Carabao Cup that helped City reach the final and eventually win the trophy against Arsenal at Wembley.

Against Wolves, Bravo made three excellent saves to keep the Blues in the competition in normal time and then saved two penalties in the resulting shoot-out with City winning 4-1.

And the Chile skipper was at it in the next round as City again went to a penalty shoot-out, saving Riyad Mahrez's spot-kick as the Blues beat the Foxes 4-3.

Bravo played every game of the Carabao Cup run and richly deserved his first winner's medal with the Blues.

Bravo also played in the FA Cup run to the last 16 and started the last two Premier League games of the season.

All in all, a solid contribution from a goalkeeper who slots perfectly into the total football ethos of Guardiola's team with his calmness and excellent distribution.

ONLY 1
CITY
20
17
18
CHAMPIONS

47

PHIL FODEN

An outstanding prospect, Phil Foden was one of the stars of England Under-17s' World Cup win, taking the coveted Golden Ball prize for good measure. Foden played 10 times in all competitions and showed why he is so highly thought of by boss Pep Guardiola with a series of impressive cameos.

PHIL FODEN	
Position:	Midfielder
Date of birth:	28 May 2000
Place of birth:	Stockport, Manchester
2017/2018	(all competitions)
Appearances	10
Goals	0
Assists	1

CITYZENS
MANCHESTER
CITY

15

ELIAQUIM MANGALA

Eliaquim Mangala left to join Everton on loan on the final day of the January transfer window, but before then he had been in and around the squad for the first half of the campaign.

He clocked 15 appearances in all competitions and was dependable and solid whenever he played. The arrival of Aymeric Laporte and return to fitness of John Stones and Vincent Kompany meant Eliaquim's first team opportunities were limited, but he was injured on his debut for the Toffees and ruled out for the rest of the season.

ELIAQUIM MANGALA	
Position:	Central Defender
Date of birth:	13 February 1991
Place of birth:	Colombes, France
2017/2018	(all competitions)
Appearances	15
Goals	0
Assists	0

PEP SAYS...

"I am really impressed with his behaviour in training. He didn't play regularly and he always accepted it and always helped us. For a manager, for the Club and for the squad environment, that is so important."

LUKAS NMECHA

With 20 goals from just 16 appearances at EDS level, Lukas Nmecha earned his first-team debut against Leicester City in the Carabao Cup and appeared again away to West Ham as he made his Premier League bow. A product of the City Academy, it was Nmecha's goals in the semi-final and final of the UEFA European Under-17 Championships that secured victory for the Three Lions. He also scored in City's penalty shoot-out win over Leicester.

LUKAS NMECHA	
Position:	Striker
Date of birth:	14 December 1998
Place of birth:	Hamburg, Germany
2017/2018	(all competitions)
Appearances	2
Goals	0
Assists	0

55

BRAHIM DIAZ

Like Phil Foden, promising midfielder Brahim Diaz clocked up an impressive 10 appearance during 2017/18. The Spanish play-maker started the season with a superb goal against Real Madrid in a pre-season International Cup game and impressed whenever he was given the opportunity. Much more to come from the exciting youngster.

BRAHIM DIAZ	
Position:	Attacking midfielder
Date of birth:	03 August 1999
Place of birth:	Malaga, Spain
2017/2018	(all competitions)
Appearances	10
Goals	0
Assists	0

Carabao ENERGY DRINK
M.C.F.C.

First silverware of the season...

Many weeks before the Premier League title was wrapped up, City secured the first piece of silverware of Pep Guardiola's tenure with a sparkling 3-0 win over Arsenal at Wembley in the Carabao Cup final.

Aside from an early scare, the Blues dominated the majority of the game with goals from Sergio Agüero, Vincent Kompany and David Silva seeing off the Gunners in style as City secured a third League Cup triumph in five years. With thousands of blue flags waving in the background, captain Kompany led City out on to the Wembley turf with the team determined to end the day with a new medal around their necks.

The Carabao Cup offered Guardiola's side the chance to secure the first available trophy of the domestic campaign and the 30,000 or so City fans inside the national stadium hoped the cobalt skies overhead were a portend of what lay ahead. The Blues began confidently with Leroy Sané and Agüero both looking sharp in attack, but it was the Gunners who should have gone ahead on eight minutes.

Jack Wilshere drove at the City defence, poking the ball through Kompany's legs before Aaron Ramsey took over, playing it to Mesut Ozil whose low cross found Pierre-Emerick Aubameyang four yards from goal – but Claudio Bravo brilliantly saved with his feet and then his hands to keep the Gabon striker out. It was a let-off for the Blues who had been caught napping somewhat, but the travelling masses behind Bravo's goal didn't have to wait much longer for the opening goal. For all City's delightful one-touch football from the back, it was a long ball forward from Bravo that caught the Gunners' rear-guard out. Agüero stood his ground on Shkodran Mustafi, then had a clear run through the middle and his deft lob over David Ospina gave the Blues the lead with 18 minutes played.

Arsenal's response was muted and there were few chances in the remainder of the half, save for a clever chip from Agüero just before the break that almost undid Ospina again. City started the second half like a side looking to wrap up the game as quickly as possible and Kompany came within a foot of doubling the lead

just three minutes in with a deflected low drive. Fernandinho had to leave the pitch through injury but the loss of the Brazilian didn't halt the momentum City were building up and just before the hour, it was 2-0. Kevin De Bruyne found Ilkay Gündogan on the edge of the box and the German's low drive was diverted home by Kompany from close range and the skipper duly set off for a memorable celebration with the City fans.

The Blues, by now rampant, attacked almost at will and on 65 minutes, the game was effectively put to bed as Danilo spotted David Silva who took the ball in his stride, glided past Callum Chambers, then slotted a low shot past Ospina for number three. So, Silva, Kompany and Agüero were on the scoresheet – all three, along with Fernandinho, the only survivors from the 2014 and 2016 League Cup successes. There were chances to further punish Arsenal in the time that remained, but the Blues had done more than enough to enjoy the last 25 minutes or so as the quest for one of the greatest campaigns in the club's history powered ahead.

VINCENT KOMPANY...

"It was funny as before the game I thought I was going to score.

"If I look at my personal situation, days like today make every minute's hard work worthwhile.

"Every chance you have you have to take and today I did it and the team did it so we are very happy."

SERGIO AGÜERO...

"For me and for the team it is always a special trophy. We are happy and I am very happy.

"It's important for us as a team and for Pep and the club to win the Carabao Cup but now we want to keep going."

PEP GUARDIOLA...

"It is important to win this trophy because our supporters are so happy.

"I'm happy for our fans, for my staff, for the players and for Sheikh Mansour and our chairman Khaldoon Al-Mubarak.

"This win is not for me, it's for Manchester City."

Premier League
Thank you
CITY
CHAMPIONS
HOWSEC
12
ROAD
SAN DIEGO

ETIHAD PLAYER OF THE SEASON 2017/18

KEVIN DE BRUYNE

A memorable season from the Belgian playmaker who has proved himself to be a world-class talent. The goals, the assists, the energy, the yards covered, the vision, the team ethic and will to win – a fantastic effort and a fully deserved win in a season of numerous outstanding candidates.

ETIHAD
AIRWAYS
PLAYER OF THE SEASON
2017 - 2018
ETIHAD
AIRWAYS
ONLY1

STERLING
7

ETIHAD GOAL OF THE SEASON 2017/18

Fernandinho's goal against Stoke City in October of last year was named Etihad Goal of the Season for 2017/18

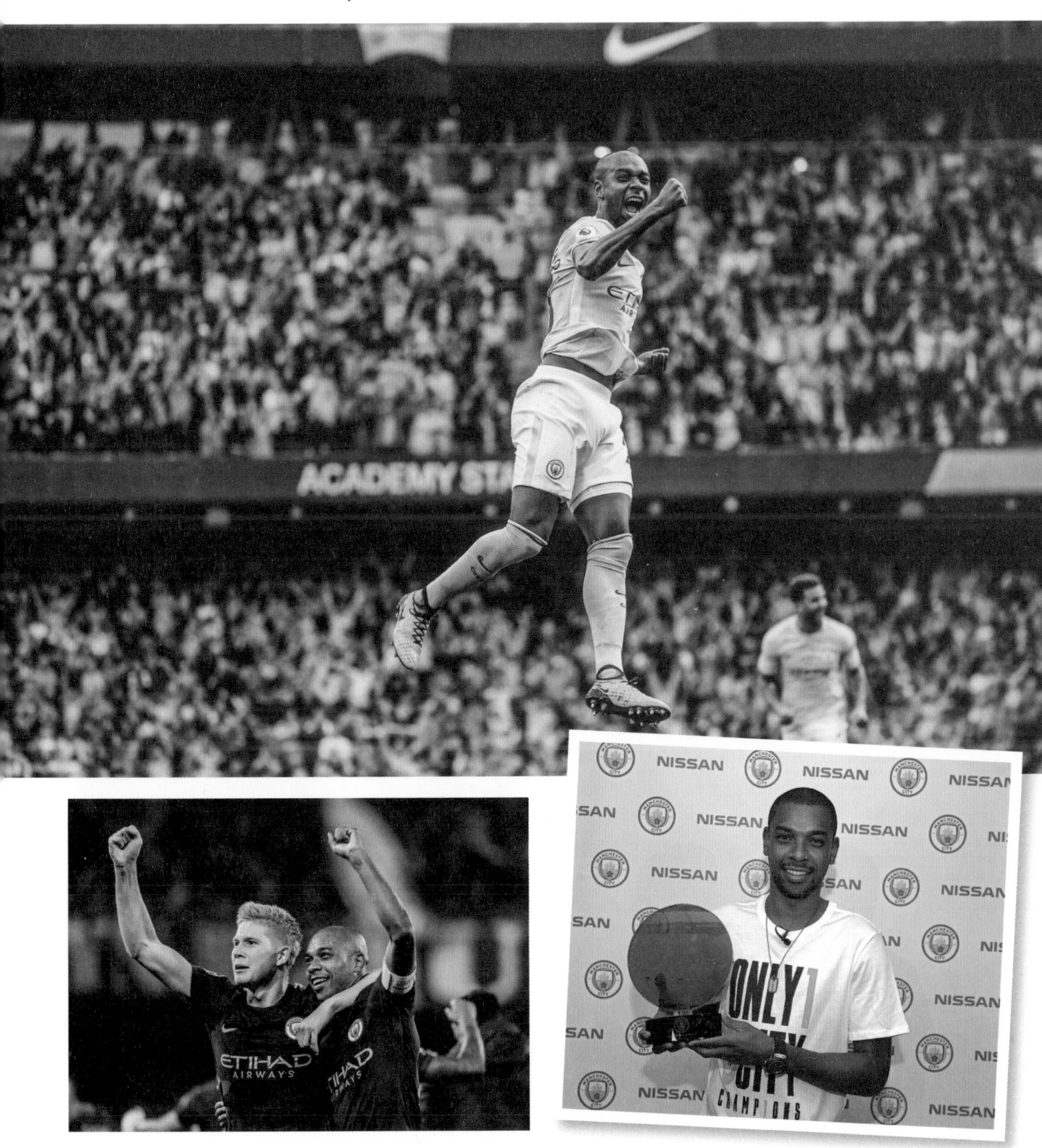

THE MANAGER, STAFF & PLAYERS

PEP GUARDIOLA

CARLES PLANCHART
LORENZO BUENAVENTURA
MIKEL ARTETA
RODOLFO BORRELL
XABI MANCISIDOR
MANEL ESTIARTE
BRIAN KIDD
DOMENEC TORRENT

SERGIO AGÜERO
CLAUDIO BRAVO
DANILO
KEVIN DE BRUYNE
FABIAN DELPH
BRAHIM DIAZ
FERNANDINHO
PHIL FODEN
ILKAY GÜNDOGAN
GABRIEL JESUS
VINCENT KOMPANY
AYMERIC LAPORTE
ELIAQUIM MANGALA

BENJAMIN MENDY
EDERSON MORAES
LUKAS NMECHA
NICOLAS OTAMENDI
LEROY SANÉ
BERNARDO SILVA
DAVID SILVA
RAHEEM STERLING
JOHN STONES
YAYA TOURE
KYLE WALKER
OLEKSANDR ZINCHENKO

Compiled from loyal fans who subscribed to #Centurions: Premier League Champions 2017/18. They take their place alongside the manager, staff and every player who contributed to our successful Premier League campaign

THE FANS

JASMICH ABIOLA
BLESSON M ABRAHAM
MARTIN ABREU
STUART ACKERMAN
JENSEN ACKERMAN
IMOGEN ADAMS
MARK ADAMS
GRAHAM ADAMS
GRAHAM ADAMS
DECLAN AHERNE
NDUBUISI AJA
PETER AKISTER
JAKE ALBISON
ROBERT ALDERSON
LANCE ALEXANDER
MARTIN ALLAN
ALAN ALLCOCK
TICH ALLEN
BENJAMIN ALLEN
DEREK ALLEN
PAUL ALLEN
HESTER ALLEN
ELIZABETH AMBERY
DOREEN AMBERY
MICHAEL O ANDERSON
MARK ANDERSON
STUART ANDERSON
JON PROSSER ANGLESEY
LUCY ANSBRO
DAVID ANSBRO
ALAN ARENSON
NICK ARMSTRONG
BRUCE ARMSTRONG
STEPHEN ARNFIELD
DIANE ARNOLD
DANIEL LUKE ARRUNDALE
MARK GEORGE ARRUNDALE
JAMES MARK ARRUNDALE
FELIX D ARSENAULT
NIGEL ASHTON
GILL ASHTON
ROBERT ASHTON
BRIAN ASSEN
THE ATHERTONS
GEORGE W ATKINSON
CRAIG ATKINSON
DOUG ATKINSON
ADAM ATWAL
WOJCIECH JAN AUGUSTYNIAK
PETER AXTON
GREG AYREY
DEREK BABILINSKI
AKASH BABU
KEN BACK
ROWLAND BAGNALL
MIKE BAGSHAW
TERENCE BAILEY
DEREK BAILEY
STEWART BAILEY
RUSSELL BAILEY
JESS BAILEY
OWEN BAILEY
JOHN BAILEY
PAUL BAILEY
DAVID BAKER
BRANDON BAKER
JOHN BAKER
MAX BALLIN
DAVE AND SUE BAMBROUGH
STEPHEN BANNER
NIGEL BANNISTER
PHILIP BARBER
RONNIE BARBER
RAY BARBER
PAUL BARBER
MARK BARBER
CHARLOTTE BARBER
MATT BARBER
STEPHEN BARDSLEY
CHARLOTTE BARKER
SIMON BARLOW
MIKE BARLOW
DEC BARLOW
SIE BARLOW
DAVID BARLOW
THOMAS BARLOW
RAY BARLOW
PETER BARNARD
LYNN BARNARD
PETER HENRY BARR
MICHAEL BARRETT
LEE BARRETT
ASH AND HUGH BARROW
DAVID BARROWCLOUGH
JAMIE J L BARSON
JAMES BARTON
ANDREW BARTON
FRANK BARTON
OTIS 'SHARK' BATE
MIKE BATES
NIGEL BATLEY
GARY BATTY
EWAN BAYLISS
DANIEL BEARD
STEFF BEARD
JOSEPH BEBBINGTON
SONIA BECKETT
SIMON BECKETT
PHILIP BEELEY
HARRY JONAS BEER
MARK BEETSON
KIMBERLY BELCHER
AMANDA BELCHER
STEPHANIE BELCHER
LEROY BELL
DAVID BELL
TY BELTON
FITZGERALD H BEMPONG
JON ATLI BENEDIKTSSON
STEPHEN BENN
GAIL BENNETT
GARY BENNETT
MARK BENNETT
JOE BENTLEY
MARTYN BENTLEY
MATT BERNARD
OSCAR BERRY
PAUL BERRY
PETER BERTHAM
WILLIAM BETTERIDGE
HARRY BETTS
ALAN DAVID BEZER
CHLOE BILLINGTON
DAVID BILLINGTON
PETER BIRBECK
ASHLEY BIRCHALL
ALEX BIRD
ANTHONY BIRD
TOM BIRD
BRIAN BIRKAN
TOM BIRTWISTLE
IAN BIRTWISTLE
JAMES ANDREW BLACK
PAUL MICHAEL BLACKSHAW
ALAN BLAMIRES
IAN BLETCHER
MALCOLM D G BLOOMFIELD
SIMON BLOW
LUKE ADAM BOARDMAN
SCOTT BOLAND
RICHARD BOLTON
SUE AND ROB BOOTH
COLIN BOOTH
BRIAN BOSTOCK
PAUL BOTMAN
HELEN BOTTERILL
TRAVIS BOULTON
ADAM BOWDEN
SIMON BOWDEN
GRAEME BOWSHER
NICK BOYD
CHARLIE BRACEWELL
PAUL BRADLEY
CAROLINE BRADLEY
PAUL ALLAN BRADY
TONY BRANTON
RAYMOND BRAY
PETE BRAZIER
TERRY BREAME
JANE BRENNER
MICHAEL BRIDGE
SIOBHAN & GRAHAM BRINE
SEBASTIAN BROCK
TOM BROCKBANK
JOHN AND EM BROCKLEHURST
DAVID BROMLEY
DAVID BROOKE
ANDREW BROOKFIELD
JOHN BROOKHOUSE
TONY BROOMHALL
PHIL BROWN
TRACEY BROWN
ALASTAIR BROWN
DAVID BROWN
PETER BROWN
MATTHEW BROWN
DAMIAN BROWN
GARY BROWN
VERONICA BROWN
EDDIE BROWNHILL
LYNN BROWNING
ROBERT BRYCE
ANDREW BRYCE
MARK BUCKINGHAM
TOM BUCKLAND
SARAH BUCKLEY
ALAN BURBIDGE
RICHARD BURCHELL
RAY BURGE
HARRY BURGESS
RAYMOND BURGESS
DANIEL BURKE
JON BURKE
JOAN BURKE
JOHN BURKE
JACK BURKE
TEZMONDO BURKE
ROB BURNS
KENNY BURNS
PETER BURT
DANIELLE BURTON
LEWIS BUSUTTIL
STEVEN BUTTERWORTH
NICOLA BUTTERWORTH
ANDREW BYRNE
BLAISE CAFFREY
STEPHEN CAIRNS
LEWIS CAIRNS
ALASDAIR CALLANDER
ANDREW CAMPBELL

SCROLL OF HONOUR

HARRISON CAMPBELL
PETER CANAVAN
PETE CANAVAN
VINCENT CANTRILL
JOHN CAREY
IAN CAREY
DALE CARLINE
ROBERT CARNEY
MICHAEL CARPENDALE
STEPHEN CARR
JOSEPH CARROLL
HELEN CARROLL
WALTER CARRUTHERS
REMY CARRUTHERS
LEE CARTER
IAN CARTLEDGE
MARK CARTWRIGHT
COLIN CATHCART
LISA CAVE
PAOLO CELESTINO
JAMES A CHADBURN
JEFF CHALLINGSWORTH
JOSHUA CHANNINGS
ROBERT CHANNINGS
JOSHUA CHATFIELD
FREDDIE CHATTERTON
SUSAN CHAUDHRY
IGOR CHECHIN
DANIEL CHEESEMAN
STEVE CHIVERS
RIC CHIVERS
FRANK CHORLEY
CLAUS CHRISTENSEN
HOUGHTON CHRISTOPHER
PAUL CIAVARELLA
JOHNNY CLANCY
PETER CLARE
MAX CLARK
GEOFF CLARKE
JOHN CLARKE
ANDREW CLARKE
STEVEN CLARKE
STEVE CLAWLEY
MARTIN MATHEW CLAY
NEIL CLAYTON
WILLIAM CLAYTON
ANDREW CLEAVER
MICHAEL CLEVERLY
TINA CLEWS
LES CLIFF
GEOFF CLOWES
REECE PETER COILS
ERIC SIMON COLDWELL
SELMA COLE
KELVIN COLES
IAN COLLINSON
JOHN CONNELL
EMILY CONNELLA
MARTIN CONNOR
DAVE SUE LOU CONNOR
ANDY CONWAY
ANN COOKSEY
MICHAEL COOKSON
DANIEL COOKSON
JOE COONEY
DAVE COOP
JOHN COOPER
STEPHEN COPE
DEAN MICHELLE CORBETT
COLIN CORBISHLEY
MARK CORNWELL
FILIPPO COSENTINO
ADAM COSTELLO
HENRY COSTIGAN
JOHN COULDING
ALAN COURSE
ANDREW COWDEN
WILL COWDEN
PHILLIP COWEY
GRAHAME COWEY
PETER COX
GRAEME COX
NATHAN COY
CRABTREE BOYS
JORDAN CRANE
VINCENT CRANE
GABBY CRAVEN
GRAHAM CRISP
RAYMOND CRITCHLOW
HOWARD CROFT
PHILIP CROMPTON
DEREK CROOK
MATHEW CROSBIE
DOROTHY CROSS
ANDREW CROSS
JAKE CROSS
SHAUN CROWLEY
ALAN CRUMLEY
STANLEY CULBERT
ALEX CULLEN
STEVEN CUMBO
JOSHUA PGM CUNDAY
VIVIAN CURNOW
PAUL CURR
OLIVER CURRAN
MICK CURTIS
ETHAN CURTIS
LES CURZON
TERRY CYMBALISTY
CHRISTOPHER D C GRYLLS
GEORGE DALY
DONNA DANIEL
RAYMOND DARKE
DOMINIC DAVENPORT
RALPH JAMES DAVIDSON
BRANDON DAVIDSON
AVA DAVIDSON
RALPH DAVIDSON
OLIVER DAVIDSON
ART DAVIDSON
ALLEN DAVIES
BILLY CHE DAWSON
PETER DAWSON
TONY DAWSON
ARJEN DE CORT
ENRIQUE DE KOEIJER
MARK DEBINSKI
JAMIE DELANEY
CRAIG DENTITH
MARK DERBYSHIRE
PHILLIP DEVENPORT
TYLER DEVINE
AARON DHANOA
STEPHEN DICKENS
PAUL DIGGETT
PETER DILLON
MICHAEL DILLON
JOHN S DINSDALE
JEAN D'IORIO
TONY DIXON
CHARLIE DIXON
SAMUEL DIXON
ALAN DODD
JAKE DODD
ELAINE DODD
JOEY DOHERTY
MATTHEW DOHERTY
CHRIS DOHERTY
JULIE DOLAN
NICK DOLAN
KEVIN DONAHUE
CAM DONALDSON
TERRY DONCASTER
GERRY DONNELLY
IAN DONNELLY
MATTHEW DONNELLY
KEN DOODSON
ANDREW DOODSON
PETER DOOLEY
ADAM DOVE
COLIN DOWDY
ZACK DOWNES
RACHEL DOYLE
PAUL A F DRINKWATER
JOHN P R DRINKWATER
PAUL DRINKWATER
KARL DRURY
PHILL DUFEU
STEVEN DUGGAN
JARED PHILIP DUMBILL
JOHN DUNLEAVY
PHIL DURBIN
BRENDAN DUTTON
THOMAS JAMES DYKE
CATHY DYSTER
JON DYSTER
JONATHAN EASTWOOD
JAN EATON
JAKE AGUERO ECCLES
KELVIN EDGAR
TONY EDGAR
MICHAEL EDMOND
TED EDMONDSON
NIGEL EDNEY
WAYNE THOMAS EDWARDS
GWYN EDWARDS
SIMON EDWARDS
DANIEL EDWARDS
ALAN EDWARDS
MATT EGGLESTON
STEVEN EGGLESTON
MARK ELLIOTT
JUNE ELLIS
ANDY ENGLAND
PAUL ENGLAND
BOBBY ENGLISH
HAROLD ENGLISH
JOHN ENTWISTLE
LUC ESPLIN
NIGEL CARR EVANS
BARRY EVANS
NEIL AND SAL EVERITT
MICHAEL FALLON
JAMES FANTON
MARK FARRAND
GEOFF FARRAR
SHAUN FAWCETT
JOHN FENNELL
PAUL FERNANDEZ
TREVOR FERREE
MICHAEL FIDLER
KEVIN FIELD
ANDREW FIELD
ERNIE FIGGINS
OMEL FIGUEROA
ANDY FILDES
RAY FILLEUL
PAUL FINERAN
AXEL CALVIN FINNEGAN
CLARE FIRTH

THE FANS

ROBERT FISH
IMMIE FISH
EDDIE FISHER
ERIC FITTON
TOM FITZGERALD
JOHN FITZSIMONS
EDWARD FLAHERTY
AMANDA FLAHERTY
PIP FLEGEL
PETER FLETCHER
PAUL FLETCHER
ANDREW FLETCHER
BILL FLINT
DECLAN FLINT
COLIN FLYNN
SHAUN FOGARTY
PETER FOGG
KENNETH FOK
AIDAN FORAN
NI FORD
AARON FORSYTH
LEE FORTH
ANDREW FOWLER
COLIN FOX
GARY FOY
RONI AND BARRY FOY
KUMBA FRANCIS
TERRY FRASER
MICHAEL FRIEDRICH
DOMINIC FRIEDRICH
THOMAS FULLER
JAMIE GAFFEY
CYRIL E GAIRY
JON GALLAGHER
PHIL GALLIER
SHAY GANDY ROYLE
JANET GARDINER
NIK GARDNER
DAVID LEE GASKELL
PETER GASKILL
TREVOR GAUNT
JILLIAN GEARY
VINNY GEE
GARRY GEE
FINLEY GEORGE
KOJO GHANSAH
MATT GIBBS
SAM GIBSON
SCOTT GIBSON
LEWIS GIBSON
GIANCLAUDIO GIGANTE
HOWARD GILBY
KEN GILLESPIE
RAY GILLESPIE
CLIVE GILLINGHAM
GEORGE GILMORE
DEAN GILMORE
DAVE OLIVER GLADDIS
CHARLIE W J GLENDON
MICHAEL GLUE
MARTIN GODDARD
ODD INGE GODHAVN
AARON GOENS
DAVE GOLDEMANN
ISAAC GOMEZ
LINDA GOODIER
PHILLIP GOODMAN
PRAVIN GORAJALA
DEREK DEKO GORDON
TASHA GOW
ALISTAIR GRAHAM HOWIE
DANIEL GRAINGER
ALEXANDER GRANDAGE
ADAM GREEN
CAITLYN GREENHALGH
EI AND STEVE GREENWOOD
MICHAEL GREGGAN
NIGEL GREGORY
KARL GREGORY
JOE GREGORY
AMY AND JOE GREGORY
PETER GREGORY
JOHN GRIFFIN
PAUL GRIFFIN
ALISON GRIFFITHS
PAUL GRIGSON
CHRIS GRIMSHAW
MATT GRONOW
GRAEME GUTHRIE
ANDREW GUTTRIDGE
DAVID GUY
LEE GWILLIAM
DR DOUGLAS GYTE
HALVOR H. HOEVRING
IAN HACKETT
JOHN STUART HADDEN
DAVID HADDOCK
DAVID BRIAN HADFIELD
LOUISE HADLEY
IAN HAGUE
C.J. HALDEMAN
PHILIP HALE
MARTIN HALL
ISABEL HALL
ANDREW HALL
GARY HALLSWORTH
ANTHONY HAMBLETON
GARETH HAMER
RYAN HAMILTON
BILL HANLEY
RICHARD HANSON
JAKE ST HARDMAN
JULIAN HARDIMAN
MARK HARDMAN
LIAM HARGREAVES
JAMES HARKER
STEVE HARKNETT
LIAM HARPER
ROBERT JAMES HARRIS
MICHAEL HARRIS
NAOMI HARRISON
MARK HARRISON
STEVE HARRISON
MICHAEL HARRISON
MARTYN HARRISS
DANIEL HARROP
NOAH HART
ROD HART
ROD HARTLEY
P AND J HARTLEY
PETER HARTLEY
GARRY HARTLEY
BARRIE HARTLEY
LINDA HARWOOD
GRAHAM HASLAM
NIK HAFIZ HASSAN
ROBERT HASTINGS
JEFF HAUGHTON
LEE LUCAS HAUGHTON
STEVE HAVENS
ALAN HAVERY
ANDREW HAWKINS
TOM HAY
ALEXANDER HAY TAYLOR
JOSEPH HEELEY
NIKLAS HEISTERHAGEN
CATO HEMMINGBY
CHRIS HEMMINGS
RICHARD HEMPSHALL
RYAN HENDRICKSON
STEPHEN HENNING
THE HENNIS FAMILY
DARREN HENSLEY
JOSH HENSLEY
ROGER HERRING
LEE HEWITSON
BRIAN HEWITT
DALE HEYS
OSCAR HICKS
JEREMY HICKS
STUART HIGGS
TERRY HILL
TIM HILTON
MATTHEW HILTON
THOMAS HILTON
KRISTIAN HILTON
ALICE HILTON
EMMA HILTON
JAMES PETER HILTON
ALAN HILTON
GARY CITYBOY HIRST
DEREK HOBBS
MATTY HODGKISSON
CHARLIE HODGSON
LIAM HOGGER
GARY HOLCROFT
DAVID HOLGATE
PAUL HOLLOWAY
GEORGE LOUIS HOLLOWAY
ALEX HOLLOWAY
CHRISTOPHER HOLMES
DANIEL HOLMES
KEVIN HOLT
KEITH HORNBY
DANIEL HORNBY
TOM HOUGHTON
RAY HOULDSWORTH
TERENCE HOWARD
DEAN HOWARTH
ADAM HOWARTH
ALAN HOWARTH
DAVID HOWE
BERNIE HOWITT
PAUL HUBY
IAN BERNARD HUDSON
PAUL HUGHES
LIAM REISS HUGHES
ROY MCFC HULL
JOE HULMES
PETER HULSE
KRISTINE HUMMEL
DAVE HUMPHREYS
MICHAEL HUNT
CHRISTOPHER HUNT BROWN
DOUG HURLEY
CHRIS HURST
WILLOW HUTTON
JEREMY HUTTON
ANNA HW
STEPHEN HYNES
ETHAN HYNES
NICK INGHAM
OLIVER INGHAM
ALFIE INGHAM
SUE AND COL INGLE
PHILIP INGLEBY
JOHN ISGROVE
SUE JACK
GRAHAM JACKSON
JAMES JACKSON

SCROLL OF HONOUR

DANIEL JACKSON
STEVE JACQUEST
STEPHEN JAMES
BILLY JAMES
LOUIS JAMES
JEREMY KEITH JAMES
GARY JANE
KRIS JANSSENS
PAUL JEFFERSON
LUCY JEFFERSON
COLIN JEFFRIES
THOMAS JENKINS
NEIL JENKINS
PAUL JENKINSON
COLIN JENKS
JULIANNA JEROME
IAN JOHNSON
PHILIP JOHNSON
JAMES JOHNSON
BRIAN JOHNSON
ADAM JOHNSON
ERNEST JOHNSTONE
OWEN JOHNSTONE
RAYMOND JOLLY
ALAN JONES
ALUN JONES
FOX AND MADI JONES
IWAN LLYR JONES
MALCOLM JONES
DANIEL JONES
STEVE JONES
IVAN JONES
RUBEN HEATH JONES
DAVE FONZY JONES
BRIAN JONES
DAVID JONES
PAUL JONES
PHILIP JONES
MADDY JONES
STEPHEN JONES
KEITH JONES
CHRIS JUDGE
LIAM JUMP
VINESH KAVASSERY
SOPHIE KAY
DAVE KEANE
EVE MCGUIRE KEANE
CRAIG KEEFE
ROSS KEEGAN
BRENDYNN KELLY
JAMIE KELLY
JACK KELLY
HARRY KELLY
MATTHEW KELLY
NEL KELVIN

RON KENDAL
ROB KENDAL
JON KENNY
CHARLENE KENYON
JOHN KEOHANE
GRAHAM M KINDER
ADRIAN KING
DEREK KING
LEANNE KING
DENIS KINNEALY
SARI KINNUNEN
ADAM KIRK
ZAK KITCHINER
DAVID KNIGHT
ROBERT KNOTT
LOUIS KNOWLES
DAMON KOULOURIS
EDWARD KOZACZEK
STUART KRAUSHAAR
JOHN GALAHAD LAING GIBBENS
DAVID LANCASTER
MICK LANE
ANGELA LANE
OLLIE LANGDOWN
GABRIELLE LANNON
PATRICK E LANTRY
RICHARD LANTTO
NIGEL LAVERICK
SEAN LAVERICK
BOB LAW
TOMMY LAYCOCK
AIDEN LE SAINT
MICHAEL LEACH
JOHN LEANE
KIERAN LEANE
KEVIN LEATHER
BEN LEATHER
ANDY LEATHER
FELIXOLIVIER LEBLANC
PAUL LEE
DAVID LEE
BEN LEE
SAMUEL LEE
JENNY LEES
XU LEIYANG
JS THOR LEMIEUX
TOM LENTON
ALAN LENTON
STEVE LEONARD
MICHAEL LEVI
ALEXIUS LEWCZUK
DEREK LEWIS
DAVE LEWIS
PHIL LEWIS
JULIE LEYLAND

ETHAN LINAKER
COLIN LINDLEY
ALAN LINGARD
BLAKE LINLEY
ALEC T DAVID LITTLEFAIR
NATHAN LLOYD
ALEX LOCKHART
ARCHIE LOCKWOOD
ANTHONY LOMAS
MATTHEW LONGDEN
MARKJIMCHAZ LONGDEN
IAN CTID LONGSHAW
CHARLOTTE LORD
BILL LOWE
STEVE LOWNDES
BRIAN LOWNDES
RAY LOWREY
MARY E LUCAS SMITH
STEVEN LUMB
LISA LURRING
JOHN LYNCH
JOSHUA LYNE
RICHARD LYNHAM
RUTH LYON
STE AND JOE LYONS
JAKE MABBUTT
ANDY MAC TRUE BLUE
BIG LEE MACBETH
DUNCAN MACFARLANE
JOHN MACHIN
SCOTT MACKENZIE
JAMES BRIAN MADDISON
HARRISON MAGUIRE
BRENDAN MAHER
ROBERT MAJEWSKI
LAWRENCE MALCZAK
GRAHAM MALIN JR.
ANDREW MALLANDAINE
PAUL MALVERN
MADAN MANANDHAR
SPIKE MANCINI
PHIL MANFORD
JOHN MANNING
LIAM MANSON
DAVID MARFLEET
HAYLEY JANE MARSDEN
CHRIS MARSH
HARRY MARSHALL
NEIL MARSHALL
HAROLD MARTIN
SCHOLLY MARTWICH
ADAM MARYCZ
MIKE MARYCZ
CALLIE MARYCZ
JULIE MARYCZ

ARRAN TRACY MASON WRIGHT
NEIL MATHER
MICAH MATTES
NIA MATTHEWS
SHAUN MATTHEWS
ETHAN MATTHEWS
PATRIK MAUER
LUCAS MAUND
CHRISTOPHER MAWN
DEBORAH MAXWELL
COLIN MAXWELL
JASON MAYALL
CONRAD MAYALL
PAUL MAYMAN
BEN MAYNARD
JAMES JOSEPH MCADAM
EDDIE MCCABE
BRIAN MCCALLIN
LUKE MCCANDLESS
ELLIOT MCCARTHY
ANDREW MCCONNELL
DARREN MCCULLOUGH
RONNIE MCDONALD
SHAUN MCDONNELL
MILO MCDONNELL
CATHRYN MCDOWELL
ANYA MCGIBNEY
PAUL MCGOVERN
KEVIN MCGOVERN
MICK & LIZZ MCGOWAN
BILL MCGUINNESS
SHARYN MCGUINNESS
STEVE MCHALE
MARK MCKAY
ANDREW MCKENZIE
ALEX MCLAGGAN
JOHN PAUL MCLOUGHLIN
JOHN MCLUCKIE
LIAM MCMAHON
JAMES MCMULLEN
MATHEW MCNEIL
COLIN MCNEILLIE
PADRAIC MCPARTLAND
STUART MCVEAN
LISA MEALING
PAUL MELLOR
STUART MELLOR
ETHAN MELLOWS
FRANCIS MELODY
DAVID MEREDITH
CHRISTOPHER METCALFE
PAUL METZINGER
BRENNAN MICHAEL
BECKY MIDGLEY
DIOGO MIGUEL

THE FANS

DAVID JOHN MILES
EDDIE MILES
JULIE MILES
ALAN MILLBERY
JULIAN MILLER
JIMMY MILLER
ROBERTO MILLIAMS
ELLIOT MILLS
ROY MILNE
MIKE MILNE
MICHAEL MILNE
PETER MIRCZUK
BETH MIRFIN
STEPHEN MITCHELL
BRENDAN MITCHELL
KARL MITCHELL
CAROLINE MITCHELL
CAROLYNE MIZRACHI
AALIYAH MOHAJERI
TIMOTHY MOK
EMMA MOLLOY
GARY MOORE
KAREN MOORE
SIMON MOORE
GRAHAM MOORES
NICHOLAS MORAN
ANTHONY MORAN
BARBARA MORETON
BENJAMIN MORGAN
JOHN MORGAN
CATHERINE MORGAN
DANIEL MORGAN
TOM MORIARTY
SUE MORRIS
MALCOLM MORRIS
JOSEPH NIALL MORRIS
CHRIS MORRIS
MICHAEL MORRIS
MARIA MORTIMER
DAVID MOSS
MARGARET MOUATT
ANDREW MOVERLEY
TOMMY MUIR
ALAN MUIR
LEE MULLARKEY
RICHARD MULLEN
SAM MUMFORD
KEITH MUNRO
SHAUN MURPHY
GARY MURPHY
JJ MURPHY
PADDY MURRAY
OLIVER NAGLOST
WILL NAJARIAN
CHRIS NATT

RUSS NEIL
JOAO NEIVA
JACK NESBIT
KEV, LEE, CAL, JOE LB NEWBURN
TONY NEWGROSH
PETE AND VAL NEWTON
RAY NEWTON
STUART NODEN
PATRICK NOLAN
DAVID NOLAN
COLIN NOON
KYRAN NOONE
ADAM NORRIS
PHYLLIS NORTON
JAMES NORTON
NINA NOVAKOVICH
SAM K NTI JR
WAYNE NUTTER
KEITH OATES
COLIN O'CONNOR
KIERAN O'CONNOR
MAURICE O'CONNOR
TERRY O'DONNELL
ALFIE OGDEN
FAITH O'GRADY
ROSIE O'GRADY
JOHN OLDRIDGE
RICHARD OLIVER
TOMOKO OLLIVANT
DES O'NEILL
KEVIN O'REILLY
EMMA O'REILLY
JOHN O'REILLY
THOMAS O'REILLY
NIGEL ORMEROD
SAMUEL ORMESHER
KEVIN OSBORNE
GODFREY OSSACK
TONY OSTELL
MATTHEW OWEN
PETE OWEN
AYAKO OZAWA
DARREN PAGE
DEBORAH PAGE
BRIAN PALMER
TREVOR PALMER
SHAUN PARKER
ERROL PARKER
MARTIN PARKER
JAGO PARKER
RICHARD PARKINSON
FREDDIE PARKINSON
DARREN PARNELL
JOHN PARR
JACOB PARTINGTON

JAYANT PATEL
SUSAN PAYNE
TONY PEAKE
MARK PEMBERTON
HARRY PERFECT
CHRIS PERKINS
PATRICIA PERKS
COLETTE PERRY
MICHAEL PETERS
AIDEN PFEIFER
ANDREW PHANG
THOMAS PHEBY
PAUL PHEBY
ANDY PHELAN
BEN & DAN PHILLIPS
GARY PHILLIPS
MIKE PHOENIX
ANTHONY PICKERING
CHARLIE PICKERING
MIKE PICKERING
GARY NIALL PICKLES
CLIVE PICKLES
THOMAS PICKLES
JANICE PICKUP
ALAN PILLING
LOUISE PININGTON
ADAM PLACKO
MITCHELL PLATT
WILL PLUMB
BRIAN POLLARD
STUART POUNTNEY
STEPH POWELL
NIGEL POWELL
ALASTAIR POWELL
ADAM POWER
MICHAEL POWIS
MARK POYZER
ASHLEY PRACHT
CHRISTOS PRASINOS
STEPHEN PRESCOTT
TONY PRESTON
THOMAS PRINCIOTTO
BOBBY PROUDLOCK
MIKE PUNCHER
ZOE AND OTIS PUSHONG
JAMES QUIGG
PEDRO MIGUEL R BAPTISTA
HARRIS RAHIM
ADIL RAJA
KYLE RASMUSSEN
PETER RAWLINSON
SAM RAYNER
ANN RAYNER
JAMES DANIEL RAYNOR
JULIE READING

JULIAN RECTO
NIALL REDFERN
JENSEN REED
ALUN REES
DAVID REEVES
ELAINE REEVES
WILLIAM REGAN
CHRIS REILLY
RICHARD REMMERT
GEORGE RENSHAW
MIKE.SHEILA REYNOLDS
TAIYSE RICH
BARRY RICH
GARY RICHARDS
JOHN RIDGWAY
SEAN JANE RILEY
GRANT RITCHIE
JAMIE RITCHIE
MILES JAMES ROACH
RHEON A ELIS ROBERTS
KEVIN ROBERTS
BEVERLEY J ROBERTS
CHARLIE ROBERTSON
DENNIS ROBINSON
MATTHEW ROBINSON
DAVID ROBINSON
JACK ROLFE
NATHAN ROLFE
JONATHAN ROPER
JIMMY ROSE
MICHAEL ROSE
ETHAN ROTHE
T ROTHWELL
STEVEN ROUGHSEDGE
DOUGLAS ROYLE
PAUL RULEMAN
WILLIAM RUSSELL
TERRY RUSSELL
PHILIP RUTTER
WILLIAM RYAN
SAM RYAN HALBERT
ARCHIE SADLER
PAUL SAFA
JACOB SAFA
NEIL SALTMARSH
NIGEL SAMBROOK
HENRY SANDERSON
DAVID SANKEY
LUKE SAUNDERS
MIKE SAUNDERS
PETE SAUNDERS
GERARD SAVAGE
BEN SAVAGE
JOE MICHAEL SAVORY
ROB SAXON

SCROLL OF HONOUR

MARTYN SCALES
VINZENZ SCHNELL
MARK SCHOFIELD
DAVID SCHOFIELD
DAN SCHOLEY
MARK SCOTT
STEWART SCULL
ROBERT SEABRIGHT
JOHN SEAL
MARK SEAL
JONATHAN SEALBY
DAVID SEALE
CRAIG SEERS
ANDREW SEERS
PAUL SEERY
OLA SETSAAS
ANDY SEWART
MARTYN SEYMOUR
PAUL SEYMOUR
SEAN SEYMOUR
MARILYN SHACKLETON
DEREK SHANKS
MARTIN SHARKEY
ANDREW SHARP
NEIL SHARPLES
JONATHAN SHAW
MICHAEL SHAW
DAVE SHAW
ANTHONY SHER
REENO CHE SHERRATT
GEORGE SHERWOOD
DAVID SHONE
HUCKLEBERRY SHUTTLEWORTH
NIKOLAS SILIKAS
LUKE SILVESTER
ANDREW SIMANIS
MICHAEL SIMMONDS
PAUL SIMMONDS
CLIFFORD SIMPSON
CHRISTOPHER SIMPSON
JANE SIMPSON
ZARA SINARAHUA
ANGELA SINGH
PHILIP SINGLETON
PAUL SKELTON
GORDON SKINNER
VAL SLATER
JOHN SLEEMAN
MACKENZIE SMALLMAN
GRAHAM SMITH
DAVID MARK SMITH
DAVID SMITH
DAVID JOHN SMITH
COLIN SMITH
MIKE SMITH
STANLEY SMITH
CAIN SMITH
KATHARINE SMITH
MALCOLM SMITH
ANTHONY SMITH
LEONIE JADE SMITH
HARRIS SMITH
CHARLIE SMITH
NEIL SMITH
KEITH SMYTHE
JOE SNELLIN
NEIL SOANES
STEIN SOERNSEN
SANNA SOERNSEN
OCTAVIAN SOKOLOW
ANDREW SOUTAR
HENRY SOUTH
CHRISTOPHER SOUTHWARD
BEN SPANTON
ROBERT DAVID SPARROW
RICHARD SPENCE
JOHN SPENCER
DANIEL SPOONER
COLIN ST JOHN
BEN STAFFORD
STEWART STAFFORD
ADRIAN STANNERS
STEVE STARKIE
LEWIS STEELE
OLIVIA STELL
THOMAS STENTON
ADAM STEPANEK
TOM STEPHENS
NICK STEPHENS
NIKKI STEPHENSON RIP
TANEISHA STEVENS
ALFRED STEWART
NATHAN A STEWART
ANNE STOCKDALE
GENE STRAHAND
MICHAEL STRAHAND
RICHARD STRAW
GRAHAM STRICKLAND
TIM STROGUSZ
MCLAUCHLAN STUART
IAN STUCHBURY
GARY SULLIVAN
JOANNE SUMMERFIELD
DEREK SUMMERS
COLIN SURREY
MO SURREY
BETSY HOPE SUTCLIFFE
KNUT ERIK SVENDSEN
WAYNE SWANN
GEORGE SWANN
DOMINIC SWARBRICK
MEGAN SWEENEY
BERNARD SWINBURN
RODNEY SYKES
SYKESY AND GEORGE
NICHOLAS TAAFFE
CHRISTOPHER TANTILLO
MIKE TAYLER
JAY TAYLOR
RIVER TAYLOR
PAUL TAYLOR
KENNETH TAYLOR
LEE TAYLOR
DARREN TAYLOR
CLAIRE TAYLOR
GARY TAYLOR
MARCUS TAYLOR
MARK TAYLOR
ANDY TAYLOR
WILLIAM TELFORD
NEIL THIRLWAY
ETHAN THOMAS
ALFRED THOMAS
PHILIP THOMAS
PETE & JOSH THOMAS
GEORGE THOMPSON
JOHN THOMPSON
NIGEL THOMPSON
DAVID THORNLEY
TIM THWAITES
SIMON TILLEY
MATTHEW TIMMINS
DANIEL TIMPERLEY
STEPHEN TIVNAN
PATRICK TIVNAN
HOWARD TOMLINSON
ROBIN TOMPKINS
PAUL TOOVEY
VI TRAN
KEN TRAVIS
GRAHAM TRAVIS
TONY TRIMINGHAM
SILAS TUCKER
COLIN TURNER
GARRY TURNER
JEFF TURNER
NEIL TURNER
DAVE TURNER
STUART JOHN TURNER
CONNOR TURNER
PETER TURNER
NICHOLAS TURNER
JOSEPH TURNER
SUE TURNER
SARAH TURNER
MARCO TUZZA
SAM TWEEDIE
ALEC UREN
DAN USANSKY
MANSOUR VAFAIE
OSCAR VAN DIJK
WILLIAM VENEZIA
ALEXIS VENTURA
COLIN VICK
VARUN VIJAYAKUMAR
CHRISTOPHER VINCENT
SAM & THOMAS VINCENT
SHIRLEY VISCO
ARTHUR WADE
ERIC WAGHORN
JASON WAGNER
IAN WALKER
DAVID JOHN WALKER
BRUCE WALKER
ROB WALKER
VINCENT WALKER
JAMES WALLACE
CAMERON WALLACE
WILLIAM L WALSH
COLIN WALTON
JACKIE WALTON
NURULAMIN WAN HUSSIN
DIDS WANATH
BEN WARD
CHRISTINA WARDEN
LEE MICHAEL WARDLE
NORTON WARDLE
DAVID WARNER
WILLIAM WATKINSON
DAVE WATKINSON
CARL WATTS
ROY WEBB
DARRELL WEBB
MILES WEBBER
KATY WEBSTER
GARY WEIGHTMAN
DAVE WELCH
SUE WELCH
CHRISTOPHER WELLENS
LEE J WELLENS
HENRY WELLS
ALEX WESTBROOK
JAMIE WHELAN
ANDREW WHELAN
MICK WHILEY
GREG WHITE
JOSHUA WHITE
PAUL WHITE
DARREN WHITE
JANET WHITE

THE FANS

MICHAEL WHITE
JULIE WHITEHEAD
ADRIAN WHITEHURST
JASON WHITNEY
STEVEN WHITTAKER
JONATHAN WILD
RICHARD WILD
HARRISON WILDE
MICHAEL WILDMAN
ADAM WILDMORE
MICHAEL WILEMAN
PETER WILHELMSSON
JOSHUA WILKEY ARNOLD
JAKE WILKINSON
NIGEL WILKINSON
RACHEL WILLCOCK
PHIL WILLIAMS
BARRIE WILLIAMS
SCOTT WILLIAMS
KYLE WILLIAMS
STEPHEN WILLIAMS
SION ARWYN WILLIAMS
JOE AARON WILLIAMS
SUSAN WILLIAMSON
STEVEN WILLIAMSON
DAVID WILLIAMSON
COLIN WILLIS
TIM WILLITTS
BEV WILSHER
JOHN WILSON
CRAIG WILSON
GARY WILSON
MICHAEL WILSON
ZACK WILSON
COLIN WILSON
STUART WILSON
PETER WILSON
RALPH WILSON
MARY WILSON
RAY WILSON
JOHN C WILSON
STEVEN WILSON
LYNDON WILSON
STUART WILTON
VINNY WINN
LEAH WINSTANLEY
ANDREW WINSTANLEY
DANIEL WINWARD
COLIN WITCHARD
ISAAC WITHEY
RICHARD WITNEY
MATTHEW WOOD
ALEX WOOD
JOHN WOOD
NICK WOOD
GEOFF WOOD
JULIAN WOOD
MICHAEL JOHN WOOD
STEVE WOODBRIDGE
MIKE WOODCOCK
DAVID WOOLLISCROFT
DEBBIE WOOLLISCROFT
DAVE WOOLLISCROFT
GLYN WORRALL
MARK WORSNIP
GREG WORSWICK
MARK WORTHINGTON
ANDY 'CITY 69' WRAGG
SAM WRIGHT
BRENDA WRIGHT
DAVID T WRIGHT
DEREK WRIGHT
JOHNNY WRIGHT
HARRY WROE
STEPHEN WROE
BARBARA WUJUKLIDIS
MATT AND TOM YATES
MARCUS YATES
FRED YATES
JAMES YOON
EATON BLUE YOULD
TOMOKO ZAITSU
FIN ZARTARIAN
P S G N ZELENOVIC
ANDREAS ZELLER

PREMIER LEAGUE TABLE 2017/18

Team		Pld	HOME					AWAY						
			W	D	L	F	A	W	D	L	F	A	GD	Pts
1	Manchester City	38	16	2	1	61	14	16	2	1	45	13	79	100
2	Manchester United	38	15	2	2	38	9	10	4	5	30	19	40	81
3	Tottenham Hotspur	38	13	4	2	40	16	10	4	5	34	20	38	77
4	Liverpool	38	12	7	0	45	10	9	5	5	39	28	46	75
5	Chelsea	38	11	4	4	30	16	10	3	6	32	22	24	70
6	Arsenal	38	15	2	2	54	20	4	4	11	20	31	23	63
7	Burnley	38	7	5	7	16	17	7	7	5	20	22	-3	54
8	Everton	38	10	4	5	28	22	3	6	10	16	36	-14	49
9	Leicester City	38	7	6	6	25	22	5	5	9	31	38	-4	47
10	Newcastle United	38	8	4	7	21	17	4	4	11	18	30	-8	44
11	Crystal Palace	38	7	5	7	29	27	4	6	9	16	28	-10	44
12	Bournemouth	38	7	5	7	26	30	4	6	9	19	31	-16	44
13	West Ham United	38	7	6	6	24	26	3	6	10	24	42	-20	42
14	Watford	38	7	6	6	27	31	4	2	13	17	33	-20	41
15	Brighton & Hove Albion	38	7	8	4	24	25	2	5	12	10	29	-20	40
16	Huddersfield Town	38	6	5	8	16	25	3	5	11	12	33	-30	37
17	Southampton	38	4	7	8	20	26	3	8	8	17	30	-19	36
18	Swansea City	38	6	3	10	17	24	2	6	11	11	32	-28	33
19	Stoke City	38	5	5	9	20	30	2	7	10	15	38	-33	33
20	West Bromwich Albion	38	3	9	7	21	29	3	4	12	10	27	-25	31